Flow
The 1949 Murder of Dana Marie
Weaver in the "Star City" Roanoke,
Virginia

Denise Tanaka

with contributions from Laurie Platt

Published by Sasoriza Books

Published by Sasoriza Books
www.sasorizabooks.com
https://www.facebook.com/SasorizaBooks
Cover design by Elina

Acknowledgments

FIRST, I WANT TO THANK Laurie Platt for reaching out to me with the idea for this project. For many years, Laurie has been hoping for a book to be written about this incident. Throughout our collaboration, she provided insights into the community as well as valuable research sources. Born and raised in Roanoke Virginia, she is the owner of two dogs Charlie and Sadie.

Our sincere appreciation goes to the staff of the Roanoke Public Library, Virginia Room, and to all the reference librarians of the South County Library system, for providing us with resources and information about this case.

We are very grateful for the generous assistance of Kevin Shupe, Senior Reference Archivist at the Library of Virginia. He went above-and-beyond in efforts to uncover a treasure trove of unpublished documents from the Virginia State Penitentiary and the Governor of Virginia's executive pardon records.

DENISE TANAKA AND LAURIE PLATT

Dedicated to the alumni of Jefferson High School

4

Prologue

I WAS FIRST APPROACHED about this project by Laurie Platt, a long-time resident of Roanoke, Virginia, who wanted to tell the story of the most notorious murder case in the town's living memory. When she was a small girl, Laurie's mother sternly warned her to *never* go into a church alone. Curiosity lingered for years until she later figured out the connection. A teenaged girl was murdered in 1949 before Laurie was born. This brutal crime shocked and horrified the city, making headlines at a time when the nation was struggling to recover from the horrors of World War II and dealing with the new fears of nuclear destruction in the Cold War era. The murder happened in the one place a girl should have felt safe: in a church.

The trauma of this girl's tragic death cut deeply into the hearts of those who experienced it first-hand. Unable to truly heal, even after the killer was caught and convicted, the survivors in town (like Laurie's mother) passed along their lingering trauma into the next generation. Although the crime happened over seventy years ago, to this day you can easily find people in Roanoke who remember what happened to Dana Marie Weaver.

A few articles, pulp detective magazines and vignettes have been written over the years, but no one has taken a deep dive to write a full-length book about what happened. While conducting research for this project, Laurie found it hard to reach anyone who wanted to be interviewed and share their memories. The victim's high school classmates rarely spoke of the incident as the years passed. By now, they have all aged into their nineties or passed away. Laurie's neighbors and Facebook friends, one after another, responded with the same refrain. *Let it go. Don't bring it up. Let the past stay in the past.*

Denial is the first defense mechanism that our brain uses, automatically and unconsciously, to distort sensory information and interpret unpleasant facts into less threatening memories. Everyone does it. No one enjoys looking straight into the face of what we fear. We may not choose consciously to be in denial, yet our brains protect ourselves from being overwhelmed with painful emotions. As the playwright Tennessee Williams wrote in *The Glass Menagerie,* "Memory takes a lot of poetic license. It omits some details; others are exaggerated, according to the emotional value of the articles it touches, for memory is seated predominantly in the heart."

Avoiding painful truths comes with a cost. By failing to face problems head-on, we deprive ourselves of learning constructive lessons that could improve our lives or potentially benefit others. Suppressing painful feelings does not mean they go away; they stay in our unconscious like a plastic container full of rotting food at the back of the refrigerator. An unintended consequence of denying painful feelings is depression, becoming numb to the joys of life and perhaps even love. Energy that could be used constructively or creatively gets channeled sideways into holding down a lid on those painful feelings.

My wish here is not to stir up unpleasant matters that will upset people for the sake of publicity and exploitation of tragedy. I agreed to collaborate with Laurie on this project for the sake of telling the truth. So, dear reader, you will not find here a titillating "true crime" book full of sensationalized, tabloid details. There are no gory crime-scene photographs. This chronology of events includes an exploration of the historical context and sociological factors that surround the case.

My goal in telling this story is to explore the humanity in what lies beyond the newspaper headlines. What was in the heart of the killer, the victim, the witnesses, and all the rest who felt touched by this tragedy? I have never lived in Virginia and never knew about Dana Marie Weaver until Laurie Platt contacted me. My personal connection to Roanoke is that one of my ancestors (named Lizzie Wilson) was brutally killed in a random act of violence over a hundred years ago. My distant relative is buried in Roanoke's City Cemetery on Tazewell Avenue. To this day, Lizzie's murder is unsolved. My elder relatives rarely spoke of it over the years, and so I understand all too well how a family's pain can be suppressed but never truly healed.

Hopefully by looking back at what happened with a clear eye, I can perhaps offer solace and comfort to this wounded community. My prayer is that, after all these years, Dana Marie and her killer Lee Scott can both finally rest in peace.

Chapter 1. Discovering the Body

ALEXANDER R. ROLAND never imagined that he would be the one to discover the body of a murdered girl. Up until the morning of May 9, 1949, the custodian of Christ Episcopal Church had led a fairly anonymous, uneventful life. That suited him just fine.

Early on that Monday morning, Mr. Roland got out of bed and made ready to go to work. He was a widower in his early fifties, having lost his wife Carrie Bell Flowers at some point in the last five years. Originally from Birmingham, Alabama, now he lived alone in Roanoke, Virginia, a major city and railroad hub in the Blue Ridge Mountains region.

As an African-American man, he had no choice but to make his home in the northwest quadrant of the city. Roanoke was strictly segregated along black-and-white racial lines, with clear boundaries for where its residents could (or could not) buy or rent homes. Mr. Roland lived on the other side of the railroad tracks that bisected the city from east to west, but he may as well have lived on another planet.

His life up until that point was fairly typical and uneventful. As such, for many reasons it is difficult to find his paper trail in the usual genealogy websites and public records. For insight into what brought Alexander Roland to this place on this day, we need only look at the historical context. His experiences were shared by thousands upon thousands of men his age.

In 1949, the southern states kept its black and white residents restricted by laws, both written and unwritten, during what is known as the Jim Crow era. This racial caste system operated in full-force for roughly one hundred years between the mid-1870s (following the end of the Civil War) up until to the mid-1960s with the Civil Rights era. The Thirteenth, Fourteenth, and Fifteenth amendments to the U.S. Constitution granted African-Americans freedom from enslavement, full citizenship, the right to vote and other legal protections. However, the so-called Jim Crow laws in resistance to progress sprang up swiftly at the city and state level. As the saying goes, two steps forward and one step back.

Around the time that Mr. Roland was born, the U.S. Supreme Court in 1896 issued its landmark decision in the case of *Plessy v. Ferguson* which sustained the constitutionality of the Jim Crow ideology. States were given free rein to enact widespread "separate but equal" laws that restricted African-Americans from riding in certain seats of public transportation, that prohibited attending certain public schools, eating at whites-only restaurants, using public toilets or drinking fountains, or buying homes in certain neighborhoods. An entire infrastructure developed of whites-only or blacks-only facilities such as separate hospitals, prisons, schools, churches, and even cemeteries. In many places, there were no black facilities at all—no public restrooms and no designated areas of city parks where African-Americans were allowed to sit.

One prime example of segregation's negative effects is the story behind one of Roanoke's hospitals. Until the early 20th century, there were no hospitals in southwest Virginia that offered services to anyone who was not considered white. Dr. Issac David Burrell was an African-American physician working to establish a hospital in Roanoke to serve his community. Before his dream could be realized, he fell ill with gallstones and urgently needed surgery. None of the whites-only hospitals in the area would provide him with care. He was forced to travel several hours to Washington D.C. for treatment, riding in a train's baggage car. The delay cost his life. The heart-wrenching circumstances of his death served as a catalyst to ensure that this tragedy would not be repeated for another person. Burrell Memorial Hospital, named in honor of Dr. Burrell, opened in 1915 on Henry Street in the northwest quadrant of Roanoke. In 1921 the hospital moved to a new location at 611 McDowell Avenue N.W. where it stands today.

Alexander Roland's ancestors—their names lost to the passage of time—were enslaved like so many others brought from Africa against their will. His forebearers may have lived in America for hundreds of years but his family tree was shattered. Unable to legally marry... Unable to prevent their children from being sold at auction like livestock... The majority labored in the farm fields of the southern United States up until the Civil War in mid-1860s when slavery was abolished. His own father William "Reed" Roland was born less than a year after the Confederate Army's general Robert E. Lee surrendered to the head of the Union Army General Ulysses S. Grant on April 9, 1865 at the Appomattox Court House in Virginia.

Records are hard to find for African-Americans in this period of history. I can only speculate that Mr. Roland's grandparents and his parents endured the tumultuous period of Reconstruction and the beginnings of the Jim Crow era. His father Reed Roland at the age of 35 was too deep in poverty to rent a roof over his own head. The 1900 federal census of Birmingham, Alabama shows him as a widower residing alone in an almshouse. A death certificate for his wife (Alex Roland's mother) Jenny Gardner has yet to be found, much less the cemetery where she is buried.

Alexander Roland worked in factories doing menial labor throughout his life growing up in Birmingham, Alabama according to U.S. census records that list each person's occupation. When his wife died and World War II ended in the mid-1940s, he moved to Roanoke, perhaps to be nearer to his younger brother. The Reverend William Robert Roland (last name alternately spelled Rollians) made a decent living by making and selling medications. He and his wife Verna operated the Rollians Drug Store in downtown Roanoke for several years. A resident of Roanoke since the late 1930s, Rev. Rollians was also a minister preaching the Gospel of the Lord at the Baptist church.

Yet, to be a black business owner in Roanoke in those days was the exception rather than the rule. Employment prospects in Roanoke were limited mostly to unskilled day labor, the lower-paying jobs at the railroad's machine shops, serving meals to white passengers aboard the passenger trains or to guests at hotels, or a manual trade such as blacksmith or barber. Mr. Roland found an honest day's work serving as the custodian at Christ Episcopal Church—a church where he had the privilege of keeping the building clean but could not attend the worship services himself. Of course he went to work in the early hours of a Monday while no one else was there. No one wanted to see the "colored" janitor scrubbing toilets, emptying trash cans, scrubbing yesterday's dishes, sweeping and mopping the floors.

On that fateful morning in May 1949, when Alexander Roland put on his hat and shoes to go to work, he could not know that society was on the verge of dramatic change. In just five years, the U.S. Supreme Court would issue its landmark decision of *Brown v. Board of Education* in May 1954 that ruled against the segregation of schools. Chief Justice Earl Warren famously announced that in the field of public education, the doctrine of "separate but equal" had no place. Yet the wheels of change did not begin to turn right away. It took another decade until the signing of the 1964 Civil Rights Act flying in the face of a self-proclaimed "massive resistance" by Southern lawmakers who called the *Brown* decision an illegal federal intrusion upon states' rights. A number of local city, county and state laws penalized any school district making efforts to desegregate. Public schools were shut down. Private schools sprang up. All to avoid the mandate of black and white children sharing a classroom.

In May 1949, however, changes in civil rights had not yet come. Life in general seemed to be much the same as it was the year before. A new decade—the Fifties—had yet to begin.

ALEXANDER ROLAND EXPECTED to have a quiet morning when he made the routine trip across the railroad tracks and into the southwest quadrant of town. The weather was pleasant and unseasonably warm. He may or may not have owned an automobile. If he walked (the more likely possibility) the one mile distance is about twenty minutes on foot.

He crossed a city bridge that overlooked the sprawling railroad tracks that form a wide river of gravel and iron at the heart of Roanoke's industrial core. His route took him southward along Fifth Street passing through the western end of the city's thriving downtown.

When he entered the whites-only neighborhood in the southwest part of the city, whoever else was awake at that hour made their way to work or school. Passers-by would understand that he was on temporary business to perform a menial task to cook or clean. Certainly he was not a resident; certainly he did not live there.

While making the trip from his home to Christ Episcopal Church on Franklin Road in the southwest part of town, Mr. Roland looked forward to completing his usual chores of cleaning the church building and its adjacent parish hall. He could not have imagined what he would find.

Christ Episcopal Church is a modest brick building on the corner of Franklin Road and Washington Avenue in southwest Roanoke. Originally founded in the 1890s at another location, the current building was built during World War I and opened its doors in September 1918. The worshippers who regularly gathered under this roof formed what is known as a parish—that is, a self-supporting congregation under the spiritual and practical authority of a head priest.

As is typical for many sorts of religious institutions, not unique to Christian denominations, there is a nearby building that provides space for necessary functions and social activities. For Christ Episcopal Church, the Parish House contained the administration office, classrooms, meeting rooms, and other facilities for the congregation to use outside of worship services. The chapel's main entrance lies along Franklin Road facing east. The entrance to the two-story parish house is around the corner and faces north to Washington Avenue.

At about 8:00 AM, Alexander Roland used his keys to unlock the Parish House's door. At first, everything seemed to be normal. The building was quiet and empty. He began his routine tasks of turning on the lights and moving from room to room.

He proceeded upstairs and passed through the second-floor dining hall to see if any dirty dishes were left over from the night before. Approaching the kitchen, he saw broken glass on the floor. Beyond the divided serving door, which was half open at the time, he discovered a disturbing scene. The room looked like the aftermath of a Hollywood barroom brawl showing evidence of a brutal struggle: shards of broken dishes... scattered cookware appliances... overturned chairs... misaligned tables... and blood smeared on the cabinets, the walls, and the floor. By looking over the serving door partition, he saw the slumped body of a young woman.

There was a telephone mounted on the wall in the second-floor corridor just a few feet away from the chaotic scene in the kitchen. It never occurred to Mr. Roland to call the police himself. Growing up in Alabama, the last thing he wanted to be was a man of color standing alone in a crime scene with a dead girl when police arrived. Perhaps the reasons are obvious but, even so, let us briefly digress and explore the context for this moment.

Within his lifetime, Alexander Roland may have witnessed horrific incidents or known personally the surviving family members of lynching victims. Roanoke itself was the scene of a public lynching in 1893 at the corner of Franklin Road and Mountain Avenue, ironically not far from Christ Episcopal Church's front door. The mayor and a handful of police officers had tried to defend the victim at the jailhouse, shooting into the rioting lynch mob and killing eight of their fellow citizens in the process, but to no avail. The mayor himself was chased out of town. After the lynching, the brutalization of the victim continued. The hanged man's corpse was dragged through the streets by a berserk mob and publicly burned on a pyre. This macabre carnival brought hundreds of residents into the streets to witness the spectacle and take souvenirs. This infamous so-called "Riot of 1893" was a public stain on Roanoke's reputation that city leaders worked for years to erase. Within Mr. Roland's lifetime, since the late 1930s, lynching had become a relatively rare occurrence. Of the several thousand persons brutally lynched since the end of the Civil War, the archives published on the website of the Tuskegee Institute recorded only three in the year 1949. Even so, the threat of being attacked by a lynch mob was always on a man's mind.

At seeing a dead girl in the kitchen, Mr. Roland rushed downstairs and out the door. He travelled as fast as he could to report the news to the man in charge of Christ Episcopal Church. The rectory was a residence for the rector (or priest) who had the primary authority and responsibility for the parish. The church owned the house on King George Avenue where the rector lived with his family. The distance is about half a mile or a ten minute walk down Fourth Street SW and a right turn on King George Avenue. Mr. Roland was daring to venture even deeper into the whites-only Old Southwest neighborhood.

He hurried up the footpath from the sidewalk and ascended the porch steps of the two-story, colonial style home. The large white door was framed by panes of colored glass reminiscent of the entrance to a church. He wiped his feet, removed his hat, and braced himself to knock on the door.

REVEREND VAN FRANCIS Garrett, the rector of Christ Episcopal Church, was enjoying a pleasant Monday morning so far. Perhaps he was in the middle of drinking coffee and eating breakfast with Marie, his wife of twenty-two years. I imagine he could have been reading the morning newspaper at his kitchen's dinette room, looking out at the green lawn of his back yard through double-pane French doors.

A relatively young man at forty-eight years old, Rev. Garrett had lived a very different life compared to the man who was about to knock on his door.

Rev. Garrett was a native of Williamsburg, Virginia—a town currently known for its recreation of living history as a fully functioning Colonial-era village where docents in historical costumes perform the daily tasks from a bygone era. He bore the name of his father Van Franklin Garrett and could trace the pedigree of his illustrious Garrett forefathers back several generations. He was shorter than average height for a man (at five feet and six-and-a-half inches) according to his World War II draft registration card.

He earned a bachelor's degree from William and Mary College in his hometown of Williamsburg, Virginia. The college's yearbook published his senior graduation portrait of a very serious young man in a black cap and gown. Its caption describes him in somewhat unflattering terms, one hopes in a good-natured spirit of collegial hazing. "Ladies and Gentlemen: We have before us the petite figure of Van Franklin Garrett Jr., better known around the campus as Van. He is the ladies' man of the class. Ask anybody around Tyler Hall if they know Van. He is hard to know, but once you know him you feel that he is well worth knowing. When it comes to pulling down A's in his classes, he is right there. We entertain no fear as to his future success. Here's to you, Van. We predict for you a future filled with happiness and prosperity. Don't get discouraged because you are small, for smaller men than you have often moved great mountains; we are sure of your success."

Ordained to the priesthood in 1935, he went on to gain experience teaching at high schools in Virginia and North Carolina and was director of religious education at churches in Winston-Salem, North Carolina. According to his biography printed posthumously in *The Living Church*, Vol. 146, pp. 23 (1963) he became the rector of Roanoke's Christ Episcopal Church in 1946, just three years earlier.

Reverend Garrett and his wife Marie were essentially empty-nesters. They had one child, a daughter named Josephine Yeardley Garrett, who was sixteen years old. Josephine attended a boarding school in Staunton, Virginia and so she was living away from home for most of the school year. The 1950 yearbook of Stuart Hall School published her portrait showing a hopeful young woman smiling off to the right-hand corner of the frame. The caption calls her by the nickname Jody and also engages in some good-natured, collegial hazing. "...a new addition ...never can make up her mind ...her constant companion at school—stuffed green faille pocketbook ...have a weekend, kid! ...bathing cap could sub for a sieve ...intriguing eyebrows ...always happy and singing."

On this quiet Monday morning, Reverend Garrett may have been reflecting upon what a pleasant Sunday that he and his congregation had just experienced. The day before was Mother's Day, an official U.S. holiday since President Woodrow Wilson signed a measure in 1914 designating the second Sunday in the month of May for honoring mothers and motherhood.

As recounted by Nelson Harris in his book *Hidden History of Roanoke: Star City Stories,* during the Sunday services Rev. Garrett had lectured his congregation with inspiring words about the value of family. The parish looked forward to the visit from a bishop later in the week for the dedication ceremony of a new ministry building in the city. He cancelled the weekly meeting of the Young People's Service League that regularly met on Sunday afternoons. This active, well-established group attracted participants not only from the Christ Episcopal Church parish but anyone from the neighborhood was welcome. The parish house had recreational amenities that Roanoke's wholesome youths enjoyed on a regular basis.

As a special Mother's Day treat, Reverend Garrett chaperoned his parish's youths on an excursion out of town. They loaded into several automobiles and travelled south to a location near the town of Callaway in Franklin County, roughly thirty miles away. Contemporary news reports brushed over the event, calling it simply a "picnic" but it was so much more than that. The local *Franklin News-Post and Franklin Chronicle* newspaper, in reporting on the murder a few days later, went into more detail. The location was identified as Saint Peter's-in-the-Mountains, an Episcopal church built after World War I on the site of an earlier church that was destroyed in a snowstorm. Adjacent to the church is the Phoebe Needles Mission School that originally served the rural children who could not reach the public schools in towns farther away. The school converted into a church parish house, the Center for Lifelong Learning and a summer camp operated by the Episcopal Diocese of Southwestern Virginia.

FLOWERS FOR DANA: THE 1949 MURDER OF DANA MARIE WEAVER IN THE "STAR CITY" ROANOKE, VIRGINIA

On this Mother's Day in 1949, more than two hundred fifty persons including about seventy-five of them from Roanoke gathered at St. Peter's to attend a presentation service of a Mite Box offering. This is a customary practice unique to many Christian denominations and is also known as an alms box or a poor box. In this fund-raising activity, uniquely designed cardboard boxes are circulated at special gatherings for the collection of small monetary offerings. The blue boxes are named for the story of the "widow's mite" in the Bible (Mark 12: 41 – 43) *Jesus sat down opposite the place where the offerings were put and watched the crowd putting their money into the temple treasury. Many rich people threw in large amounts. But a poor widow came and put in two very small copper coins, worth only a few cents. Calling his disciples to him, Jesus said, "Truly I tell you, this poor widow has put more into the treasury than all the others. They all gave out of their wealth; but she, out of her poverty, put in everything—all she had to live on."* The word mite is not so commonly used as it was in the days of the King James Bible translation; it refers to something very small in either size or value.

Rev. Garrett and his group of youths spent all afternoon at this excursion. In addition to the ceremonial presentation of Mite Boxes, most likely there were many other events to fill up the hours. Such a convocation of a few hundred people typically could have had activities and games for children, the singing of popular hymns led by a choir, the performance of a brass band, a parade, and an outdoor prayer service. In other words, this was no simple peanut-butter-and-jelly sandwich picnic taken on the spur of the moment.

The automobile caravan of happy teenagers returned to Roanoke from the day's outing between 7:30 and 8:00 PM. Parents picked up their children on the sidewalk steps of the Parish House. Those who lived nearby walked home in small groups, feeling completely safe on the streets of this neighborhood. Rev. Garrett lingered only long enough to tidy up his office at the end of the day. He made sure of turning off all the lights and locking up the building. In making these perfunctory rounds, he did not observe anything out of place. However, his locking-up routine did not take him upstairs to the second floor of the Parish House, to the dining hall or to the kitchen.

At the curbside on Washington Street, he waved good-night to the last of the young people meeting their parents in automobiles. Smiles exchanged all around, and the reverend went to bed thinking of what a good Mother's Day Sunday it had been.

IMAGINE THE CURIOSITY of Rev. Garrett when he heard a knock on his front door the next morning. He may have uttered the age-old question, "Who could that be?" He walked from the kitchen down the narrow foyer alongside the wooden banister of stairs leading up to the second floor. He opened the door to find the church's janitor Alex Roland standing on his doorstep, hat in hand, looking shocked and frightened.

When asked what was the matter, Mr. Roland reported the discovery of a dead girl.

Rev. Garrett telephoned the police. Then he got into his car and drove a few blocks up through town to what felt like his second home—the Church and the Parish House.

He met two officers from the city's police department, H.L. Britt and C.E. Shelor, and escorted them upstairs. There, he felt the shock and horror of viewing a crime scene. Perhaps as a clergyman he had officiated over a few funerals. He had seen lifeless bodies before but laid out nicely in a satin-lined casket, cleaned up and dressed by an undertaker. Most likely he had never seen a corpse in such a raw, brutalized state. Few of us have.

The teenaged girl had been lying dead on the floor for at least twelve hours.

A strike on the head had caused a deep cut to her scalp. Bruises stained her legs and throat. The coroner would later determine that strangulation, not the blow to the head, was the cause of death. Bits of skin were found under her fingernails, the result of when she had desperately scratched the face and arms of her assailant. Her purse, found untouched on the kitchen table, ruled out robbery as a motive for the brutal attack.

Rev. Garrett recognized the blonde girl as someone who often attended meetings of the youth social group. She was exactly the same age as his own daughter. Although she was not a member of the parish and did not come to Sunday worship services, he had seen her many times—alive.

Her name was Dana Marie Weaver.

Chapter 2. Identifying the Victim

HOW CAN WE REALLY KNOW anything about Dana Marie Weaver? Her life was cut short at age sixteen less than three months before her seventeenth birthday. She did not live long enough to swoon for Elvis Presley singing, for in 1949, the biggest heartthrob on the radio was Frank Sinatra. She did not yet wish to style her blonde hair in the fashion of Marilyn Monroe, who was a relatively unknown actress that year playing small supporting roles in a handful of low-budget comedies. Whatever sort of person she may have been in her immature, teenaged years is probably not the sort of woman she could have become. Selfish or generous... Frugal or wasteful... Loyal or fickle... No one is truly formed at such a young age. Like a flower just beginning to sprout from the soil, Dana Marie Weaver never had the chance to become an adult and make her contribution to the world.

What does someone leave behind to mark their existence? Photographs, clothing and keepsakes, personal letters, greeting cards, a journal or diary... Such things, if any existed, belong to the family. Out of respect for their privacy, the more intimate details of Dana Marie's life are best left undisturbed. Almost everyone who knew her as family or friends has passed away. Those few who survive retain sentimental memories of their childhood days more than seventy years ago.

What else remains are newspapers and scraps of public records, a high school yearbook, her death certificate and her tombstone. For a girl of sixteen, there is more of such evidence than there ever should be. Dana Marie lived in a time long before youths her age made a habit of broadcasting all the details of their lives on social media. The black-and-white television was only beginning to appear in American households. It was still three years away from privileged teenagers being chosen to dance on national television in Dick Clark's *American Bandstand* show. In 1949, only the social elites or notorious criminals got their names publicized.

On that fateful morning of Monday, May 9, 1949, Dana Marie Weaver was known only to her family, her close friends or acquaintances, and her classmates at Jefferson High School. Within twenty-four hours, her name would be broadcast far and wide as the shocking story of her murder made bold headlines from coast to coast. The newspapers published her photograph as a blonde girl smiling off to the left of the camera lens in a typical glamor-shot pose of the era. She resembled the actress Hope Lange but she was no Hollywood starlet. Her name became briefly famous for the worst possible reason.

In the days and weeks to follow her death, Dana Marie's life story would become public knowledge—everything from her extra-curricular school activities to where she last enjoyed coffee with a group of friends. The newspapers reported on her involvement with social events at Jefferson High School and, from all accounts, she was well-liked by her classmates. She chaired the committee making arrangements for an upcoming school dance. She had spent most of the day on Saturday, the eve of her murder, preparing and planning for the big event. Like most other girls her age, she eagerly anticipated the end of the school year. She looked forward to turning seventeen during summer vacation. Never could she have imagined that she would not hear the school bell ring on Monday morning.

Yet beneath her cheerful smile and active social life, Dana Marie Weaver carried an inner burden of lingering grief. Despite all outward appearances of an average middle-class upbringing, she knew hardship. She knew heartbreak. She knew tragedy.

THE FIRST BLOW TO HIT Dana Marie's family was the disintegration of her parents' marriage when she was about eleven or twelve years old. Whatever led to the failure of a twenty-five-year marriage is the family's personal affair and outside the scope of this book. To fill out the background tapestry of her short life, the juicy details of hearsay and gossip are not relevant. It is enough to know the basic facts that are available in public records.

Her father Murrell Fleming Weaver was born in West Virginia in the late 1890s as part of a large family with at least five siblings. Dana Marie's grandfather William Canaan Weaver partnered with a few of his sons in the business of buying and selling real estate in Roanoke since the 1920s. Even throughout the Great Depression of the 1930s, Dana Marie's father managed to keep a solid roof over the head of his wife and children.

Her mother Dana Myrtle Wimmer was a native of nearby Bedford County, Virginia. She had two brothers and one sister. Her family relocated to Roanoke in the early 1900s to join in the growth and development of the city. She married Murrell F. Weaver in Roanoke on April 5, 1917.

Their marriage suffered a tragedy in the early years. We can never know if Dana Marie was aware of it, or if her mother ever talked about the first-born son who only survived nine days in this world. The infant's death certificate gives his name as Billie Frank Weaver, born prematurely at seven months and passed away on September 15, 1919. One wonders if the infamous Spanish Flu pandemic may have affected her health during pregnancy or if other factors played a role in this tragedy. Two years passed before Mrs. Weaver became pregnant with another son. In all, she would raise three children.

The Roanoke City Directories (the earlier version of telephone books) record Murrell F. Weaver's residence since the early 1930s. He owned a comfortable home in the Grandin Court neighborhood, a suburban area to the southwest of the city's center. This well-defined residential community began development in the 1920s, according to information on the City of Roanoke's planning department. The area developed independently and became a part of Roanoke through a series of annexations in 1926 and 1943. Four corporate entities owned large tracts of land that eventually developed into subdivisions, schools and an office park. The majority of these historic houses, still standing, are one- and two-story brick structures that face onto streets lined with deep-rooted trees. Grandin Court's economic activity is focused along Brambleton Avenue that is a well-travelled commuter route (U.S. Route 221) into the city.

As of the 1940 federal census, the Weaver family still lived in the same home with their two teenaged boys and a seven-year-old Dana Marie. Mr. Weaver's in-laws George and Etta Wimmer shared the house, whereas ten years earlier, the 1930 federal census showed Mrs. Weaver's parents were living practically next door. Those ten years of the Great Depression must have been challenging for the family, but whatever hardships they endured, they managed to stay together.

Then came the attack at Pearl Harbor, Hawaii on December 7, 1941 and the United States entered the fray of World War II. Mrs. Weaver's two sons registered for the draft as every young man in the country was required to do. A newly-passed Selective Service Act required the registration of all young men for a draft lottery conducted on April 27, 1942. Another series of registration, known as the Old Man's Registration, collected information on the skills of men ages forty-five to sixty-four. Dana Marie's father recorded his name and personal details in this one. The second draft registration was not intended to be used for military service but to provide a complete inventory of manpower resources in the United States that could be utilized for national service during World War II. Draft registration itself did not constitute military enlistment. Once signed up, the men went home to carry on their lives. As needed, men were selected by lotteries. Every night, the young men of America listened to the radio broadcast announcements for the numbers of a lottery that few hoped to win.

While researching the lives of ordinary folks in Roanoke during the war years, I stumbled across some interesting photographs digitized in the Library of Congress Prints & Photographs Online Catalog. This series of black-and-white pictures shows schoolchildren—about the same age that Dana Marie Weaver would have been in 1942—participating in a community effort to support the war effort.

A little digging on the internet uncovered what was happening in these vignettes. During the Fall of 1942, the U.S. War Production Board issued a plan to ask America's schools to organize their students into a Junior Army for collecting scrap materials to be recycled into munitions for the war. The program was called, "Get in the Scrap: A Plan for the Organization of the School Children of America in the National Salvage Program." Approved by the U.S. Office of Education, the plan gave a system of organization for the Junior Army to the public schools in each state. The school children were granted pseudo-military ranks of Lieutenant, Sergeant, Corporal, and Private as awards for meritorious service but were not hierarchical or organizational in any way.

These school-aged Junior Commandos collected from their neighborhood all sorts of pots and pans, bicycle wheels, old stoves and Civil War cannons to donate. Kitchen fats and cooking grease were also collected to re-process into glycerin, which was in demand both as a component of medicines and for the explosive material nitroglycerin.

The scrap drives built up morale in the families at home. In the photographs of unnamed children, one can imagine how valuable it was for the children to feel useful. Instead of being helpless at home, worrying about their older brothers fighting in foreign lands, these children were given a sense of community in joining the war effort. It is easy to imagine Dana Marie Weaver as a ten year old blonde girl picking up metal objects or saving kitchen grease in the same way as her classmates were doing.

Mr. Weaver apparently deserted his wife and children at some point while the country was engaged with fighting a global war in Europe and the Pacific. His World War II draft registration card still gives the same address as his wife, but notably indicates he is "not employed." Not long after that, everything changed. The 1942 City Directory of Roanoke shows Mrs. Dana M. Weaver living alone on a cross street not far from her former home. She found a job working as a trimmer at a hat company. Mr. Weaver is nowhere to be found. So, with her two sons off fighting in the Pacific, Mrs. Weaver spent the war years as a single mother alone with only her ten-year old daughter Dana Marie at home. She worked every day to put food on the table. The Wimmer grandparents may have helped take care of the little girl after school.

Mrs. Weaver filed for a divorce that was granted, uncontested, on June 23, 1945. The one-page document claims the reason as "desertion" for over two years, recording the date of separation as March 1943. However, the court did not grant any alimony. Her ex-husband was not legally compelled to provide financial support. From that day on, Dana Marie's mother shouldered the responsibility for raising her children without a father in the house.

In those days, being divorced carried a much greater social stigma than it does today. The idea of being a teenaged girl in a so-called "broken home" living alone with her mother a "divorcee" was a difficult thing to be in the late 1940s. No doubt Dana Marie made an effort to present a happy, confident face to the world while enduring the sideways glances and whispering gossip of her classmates.

ANOTHER BLOW HIT THE family in early March 1945 with the death of Dana Marie's older brother. Murrell Reginald Weaver Jr. was born on 30 July 1922, exactly two days but ten years apart from Dana Marie's birthday. He had registered for the draft in June 1942 and went on to serve in the Pacific during World War II. While Dana Marie the "junior commando" searched her home's attic for old pots and pans to contribute to the scrap pile, she may have thought of her older brother and prayed for his safe return.

Reginald Weaver never came home; he was killed in action at the age of twenty-two on March 5, 1945 at the Battle of Iwo Jima. We do not have specific information on what her brother experienced but there is general information on the battle where he died that can give us some idea. He belonged to the 27th Marine Regiment under the Fifth Marine Division. His rank was Private First Class ("PFC") which is the second-lowest rank in the Marine Corps, ranking above Private and below Lance Corporal.

The 27th Marine Regiment was activated in January 1944 as a result of the massive increase in the Marine Corps during World War II. The regiment first saw action during the Battle of Iwo Jima on a small island in the Pacific Ocean. During the course of the battle they suffered 566 killed, 1,706 wounded, and had four Marines receive the Medal of Honor. PFC Weaver was among those who never made it home.

The Battle of Iwo Jima lasted from February 19 to March 26, 1945 and was a major victory for the Allied Forces during World War II for a strategic location in the Pacific. The U.S. Marine Corps and the U.S. Navy combined forces, landed on and eventually captured the island with its two airfields from the Imperial Japanese Army. This five-week battle saw some of the fiercest and bloodiest fighting of the Pacific War.

On February 19, 1945, the commander Colonel Thomas A. Wornham landed his troops on the island of Iwo Jima with the first waves of his regiment. He personally participated in the reconnaissance of the terrain under heavy mortar and small-arms fire. When one of his battalions was halted by enemy fire, Col. Wornham rallied his men to renew the attack and inflicted heavy losses on the Japanese soldiers.

An iconic black and white photograph known as "Raising the Flag on Iwo Jima" was taken by Joe Rosenthal depicting six Marines struggling to raise a U.S. flag atop Mount Suribachi on February 23, 1945. The photograph was extremely popular through the years, reprinted in thousands of publications. Fifty years later, a photograph of New York City fire and rescue workers posing with a flag in the rubble at the World Trade Center on September 11, 2001 echoed the image.

AS FOR MANY AMERICANS, as the decade of the 1940s came to an end, the memory of family members killed in action burned fresh in everyone's minds. While the nation strived to put on a happy face and move forward with the prosperity of peacetime, the Cold War loomed as a threatening shadow. President Harry S. Truman had signed onto the newly-formed North Atlantic Treaty Organization (NATO) only one month before Dana Marie's murder. Later in the fall, the Communist leader Mao Zedong would establish the People's Republic of China as a new country to be reckoned with. The Soviet Union tested its first atomic bomb. One year later, North Korea invaded South Korea and plunged America into another, messier military conflict. But in the springtime of 1949, Dana Marie's thoughts were occupied closer to home.

Dana Marie was in charge of maintaining a memorial display at her high school for alumni or relatives lost in the war. Many of her junior classmates shared the same experiences of older siblings who had returned from World War II either as honored veterans or honored fallen. Every day she went to classes and passed by the tribute to her brother's sacrifice. Earlier that year, Mrs. Weaver applied for a new bronze plaque to mark the grave of Murrell Reginald Weaver Jr. interred in Roanoke's Evergreen Burial Park. How could any of them have known, while placing flowers on the war hero's headstone, that the little sister would soon be buried next to him?

Dana Marie's other brother Richard Fleming Weaver was in his early twenties at the time of his younger sister's death. He attended college to earn his bachelor's degree in business with tuition paid by the G.I. Bill (a benefit paid to some of the veterans who served in World War II). He had also fought for his country during World War II and served in the U.S. Navy as a nose gunner aboard a patrol bomber seaplane. He was awarded a Distinguished Flying Cross and an Air Medal for extraordinary contributions. One can only speculate on his survivor's guilt, the fact that he came home alive when his older brother did not. Apparently, the shadow of his deceased brother the war hero loomed large in his thoughts for many years. The family's tribute in his obituary says, "he never felt like his service was worthy by comparison, and only recently began talking about it."

ON THAT FATEFUL MOTHER'S Day evening in 1949, Dana Marie Weaver's mother—a single, divorced woman—paced the floor worrying why her child had not returned home. Their modest duplex home on Day Avenue was only half a mile away from the place where Dana Marie Weaver's life ended. Mrs. Weaver worked as a secretary at Crystal Springs Elementary School and, no doubt, needed a good night's sleep to be ready for work the next day. What mother could sleep while her teenaged daughter's whereabouts were unknown in the middle of the night?

Mrs. Weaver telephoned the police at 1:30 AM to report that her daughter had not returned from the day's outings. The police made notes on the call but did not initiate a search for the missing girl. What if that officer on the night shift had taken seriously the voice of a worried mother on the other end of the phone? What if they had launched a search in the wee hours before dawn and retraced the girl's steps to her last known location? Would they have been able to discover her body a few hours earlier?

Most likely, Mrs. Weaver did not sleep all night through to the morning, until the police knocked on her door to deliver the news she had feared.

Chapter 3. Retracing the Last Steps

SUNDAY MORNING, MAY 8, 1949 was the last time Dana Marie Weaver would get out of bed and say "good morning" to her mother. Warm sunshine brightened the day. Most likely she attended worship services at the Raleigh Court Methodist Church, a parish to which her mother belonged. Streets were mostly empty of pedestrians and traffic. On Sundays it was customary for all of the schools, banks and business offices to be closed. The majority of Roanoke's citizens could be found in one of its many churches that served a variety of Christian denominations.

Perhaps Dana Marie enjoyed lunch after attending church with her mother. Her older brother Richard may have joined them. It is easy to imagine the two grown children, a teenaged girl and a college-aged young man, celebrating Mother's Day with gifts of a Hallmark greeting card, Hershey chocolates, or fresh cut flowers. Did her mother have plans for the afternoon, such as, going to the beauty salon to have a skilled professional style her hair in a permanent wave for the upcoming week? As a secretary in the office of an elementary school, Mrs. Weaver needed to look her best on Monday morning.

Dana Marie had an active social life and felt too restless to stay home all Sunday afternoon. Even if her mother owned a black-and-white television, there was not much programming yet that a teenaged girl could enjoy. Many of the iconic shows that carried into the next decade were scheduled to premiere in September 1949, but she would not live long enough to see any of them.

She had been out the day before, spending her Saturday at The Coffee Pot—a favorite place for youths to mingle. For those not familiar with the area, this landmark roadhouse is listed on the National Register of Historic Places. At the time of its construction in the mid-1930s, The Coffee Pot was the first commercial structure that one would pass along the highway entering Roanoke from the south.

The Coffee Pot is located on Brambleton Avenue in the Grandin Court neighborhood of southwest Roanoke not far from where Dana Marie lived as a child, before her parents divorced. The roadhouse was first constructed in 1936 as a gasoline filling station and tea room. Its most notable architectural feature is a fifteen-foot high novelty sculpture of a coffee pot made from stucco painted red and white, perched on the southern end of the roof. In the past, the owners arranged for steam to rise out of the spout from a furnace located in the storeroom below, bringing to life the giant percolating coffee pot. A roadhouse in the United States is the general term for a small, mixed-use premises typically built on or near a major road in a sparsely populated area that services passing travelers. Roadhouses provide food, drinks, accommodation, fuel, and parking spaces to the guests. The Coffee Pot in Roanoke has also served as a venue for musical acts, including Willie Nelson and Ritchie Valens, earning a nickname from *The Roanoke Times* as the "biggest small stage in the South." Today, this remains as the only active roadhouse located within the Roanoke Valley.

Dana Marie's companions on Saturday were a mixed group of young men and women. Along with a couple of unnamed girls her own age, the group included three older students from the Virginia Polytechnic Institute and State University (VPI) located in Blacksburg, Virginia roughly forty miles to the west of Roanoke. Today the college is known as Virginia Tech, a highly-ranked engineering college that is one of six senior military colleges in the country offering military Reserve Officers' Training Corps (ROTC) programs under the strict criteria of U.S. federal statutes. The university was first established in the early 1870s as the Virginia Agricultural and Mechanical College, and in 1944 was renamed the Virginia Polytechnic Institute. Originally an all-male institution, female students were permitted to enroll in the 1920s. In 1953, VPI would be the first public university among the eleven states in the former Confederacy to admit an African-American undergraduate.

This mixed group of high school and college students were the last people to see her alive, except for Dana Marie's killer. The newspapers withheld the identities of Dana Marie's closest companions perhaps because they were juveniles. The VPI students were named as Cynthia Parr, William Johnson, and Benjamin Richardson but various newspapers report little else on why this group of friends had come to assemble. Most likely, the college students were natives of Roanoke and had come to spend the weekend visiting their family homes.

On that Mother's Day Sunday, after church and lunch, Dana Marie left home about 3:00 PM to rendezvous with the same mixed group of friends and college students from the day before. This time, they travelled by automobile to the Andrew Lewis Tavern situated along U.S. Highway Route 11 and slightly west of the nearby town of Salem. This popular family restaurant and meeting place has long since gone out of business. Once upon a time, it was a two-story house structure resembling a country estate with two chimneys, an overhanging balcony and three gabled attic windows. In its heyday, every youth in the area enjoyed the music playing on the jukebox, ate the sizzling food cooked on a grill, or worked summer jobs waiting tables.

Could at least six or seven people squeeze into a single automobile? Back in the days of wide, sofa-like cushions and no seatbelts, a gas-guzzling sedan from Buick, Ford, Chrysler or Chevrolet could easily fit six or more youths. The group enjoyed an afternoon of talking and laughing over bottles of soda pop, hamburgers and French fries. Dana Marie may have discussed her plans, or asked advice, for the upcoming high school dance for which she was in charge of arrangements.

The group returned to Roanoke about 5:30 PM while the sky was still light. The young man who owned the automobile served as a bus driver, dropping off the other two high school girls at their homes. Dana Marie was the last passenger in the car. No doubt they offered to bring her home, expecting her to want supper with her mother. Instead, Dana Marie asked to be taken to Christ Episcopal Church where she planned to attend the weekly meeting of the Young People's Service League. In those days before cell phones and social media, she did not know the group's weekly meeting had been cancelled. She did not know that Rev. Garrett had taken the group out of town, miles away, for a special event. Apparently, Dana Marie had missed the last two meetings of the group and her sporadic attendance left her out of the communications loop.

A few minutes before 6:00 PM, the VPI students pulled their automobile to the curb at the sidewalk in front of the Parish House. They wished her well, waved goodbye and drove away. If only they had lingered long enough to escort Dana Marie up those concrete steps and into the unlocked building. They felt secure and safe in their home town. What harm could befall an innocent young

27

girl at a church, of all places? If only someone else had walked inside with her and discovered that the Parish House was not filled with a group of happy, chatting youths. In an alternate universe of "if-only" and "what if" Dana Marie might have turned around and asked for a ride home.

The college students and a few other friends made the drive back to Blacksburg, arriving on the VPI campus by 7:00 PM as the dusk began to descend in the evening sky. Little did they know, at that very moment, that their young friend was in a desperate struggle for her life. They went to bed thinking of what a good weekend it had been. They looked forward to resuming their studies on Monday morning to finish out the school year.

The church's Young People's Service League had gone elsewhere for the day. Yet the Parish House was not empty. One other person had entered the unlocked building shortly before Dana Marie's arrival. This other person belonged to the Christ Episcopal Church parish but, for some unexplained reason, did not participate in the youth group's all-day excursion. Alone, he had expected to meet a friend who never showed up. He loitered in the Parish House dining hall, feeling bored or disappointed that his buddy had failed to show. This high school boy did not plan to meet Dana Marie Weaver, had not stalked her or schemed to commit a murder. In fact, the confession to police and the courtroom testimony made it clear that he never intended to do harm to anyone that night.

Up until that night, his name and smiling photograph had appeared in the local newspapers for a reason that gave his parents cause to celebrate. A few months prior, he earned the honor of a Gold Eagle Palm. This prestigious award is given by the Boy Scouts of America to Eagle Scouts (those with a minimum of twenty-one merit badges) who are eligible to earn one Eagle Palm for every five additional merit badges earned.

In the days to come, the name of Lee Goode "Buddy" Scott would make headlines as the one who ended a young girl's life.

Chapter 4. Painting the Picture of a Boy Who Snapped

SUNDAY MORNING, MAY 8, 1949 was the last time Lee Goode Scott would get out of bed and say "good morning" to his parents without the shame of a capital crime looming over his head.

At sixteen years old, he attended the same school as the girl whose life he ended. Jefferson High School's 1949 yearbook published their black-and-white photographs, sorted alphabetically, just a few pages apart. In his portrait, Lee Scott wears a light suit and a dark tie. He smiles upward and off to the right of the frame, as if gazing hopefully into the future. Like all the other teenaged boys in his junior class, he looked forward to the end of the academic year. He would turn seventeen years old in September and had one more year until he passed the milestone of becoming an adult. Up until that fateful day, his expectations for the years to follow graduation involved applying to colleges, finding a woman to marry, and raising children to carry on the family name.

His father Norman Garrett Scott was so proud of his ancestral heritage that he bestowed his mother's maiden name as the middle name of his only son. The elder Mr. Scott made a decent living in Roanoke as an insurance salesman. They had a middle-class home on Second Street in the southwest quadrant of the city, a short walking distance from Christ Episcopal Church where the family regularly attended worship services. Mr. Scott spent his youth in a rural community near Rocky Mount in Franklin County to the south of Roanoke. At the age of twenty-one, he complied with the mandate to register for the World War I draft. That record shows that he worked for the E.I. du Pont de Nemours and Company ("DuPont") as a guncotton plant munition worker in Hopewell, Virginia. His physical description is a bit vague: medium height, medium build, with brown eyes and brown hair. After the war ended, the U.S. federal census of 1920 shows him back in Roanoke living with his family. In the 1920s, he worked with his father Ernest Lee Scott as a butcher in the city market at the heart of downtown Roanoke.

The Scott family had lived proudly in Virginia for several generations since at least the colonial era. Lee Scott's grandfather and his wife Mary Florence Goode had nine children, according to family trees published on genealogy websites. Many of the children died at a very young age. One of the adult siblings, Charles David "C.D." Scott, was a traveling carnival operator at the time he passed away. According to the index of death records for the state of Minnesota, C.D. Scott succumbed to lung cancer in 1944 at the age of forty-eight. By the time Lee Scott reached his teenaged years, his father's numerous siblings were reduced to just three sisters who had married and started families of their own.

His mother Myra Arsene Miller, originally from Indiana, married Mr. Scott on January 3, 1932 in Roanoke. Their first and only son was born in the autumn of that same year. There is a long gap of seven years until 1939 when their daughter Judith Florence Scott was born. As far as the public records show, the couple had only these two children. They called the girl Judy and nicknamed their first-born and only son "Buddy."

Mr. and Mrs. Scott felt immensely proud of both their children's accomplishments. They preserved the memorabilia of piano recitals, school report cards, and every other sort of scrapbooking keepsake that parents typically keep. Lee Scott was particularly active in school, in church, and in many extra-curricular activities. During the years of Lee's incarceration, his father worked tirelessly with a letter campaign to the governor's office and the state parole board on his son's behalf. Across several letters dated across several years, Mr. Scott repeatedly copied the same impressive list of his only son's tangible achievements:

- maintained a high grade point average at school

- elected President of his Home Room Class by the student body

- served in the Minister's Acolyte Guild at Christ Episcopal Church, after his confirmation ceremony at the age of 12; this is an organization of boys who assist at the altar during religious services

- awarded a three-year Attendance Pin for regular attendance at church; he never missed a Sunday

- YMCA boys swim coach and lifeguard; Boys Club Camp counselor and lifeguard

- played trumpet in the Junior Legion Drum and Bugle Corps

- studied piano for 5-1/2 years, attending recitals regularly

- earned the highest award from the Boy Scouts of America—the Gold Eagle Palm—as an Eagle Scout with 54 merit badges

Looking at this list, it becomes clear that Lee Scott never had a day off in his busy schedule. From an early age, every hour of every day had to be occupied with one activity or another. It is not hard to imagine that his bedroom walls showcased the framed certificates and trophy medals that made his parents so proud. His uniform for the Boy Scouts had a sash barnacled with applique merit badges and pins. One senses a theme of an overarching pressure to excel and succeed in earning tangible, public accolades. Not only did he attend classes at school, he had to be elected president of the home room and earn a high grade point average. Not only did he participate in the Boy Scouts, he had to become an Eagle Scout and earn more merit badges than any of his peers. His weekends were fully booked with piano lessons, swimming lessons, and bugle corps marching practice. Even Sundays "the day of rest" found him spending hours at church assisting on the altar or singing in the choir. The rector of Christ Episcopal Church, Rev. Van Francis Garrett, later wrote a brief testimonial letter on Lee's behalf as part of a broader effort to petition the governor for a pardon. The reverend commented that, in both the Acolyte Guild and the Young People's Service League, he was "active, and always willing to do his part whenever asked."

To the modern eye, it becomes clear that Lee Scott was under tremendous pressure to be "the best" in every activity, in every aspect of his life. His busy schedule did not allow him the leisure to sprawl on the grass among dandelions and look up at the clouds. Recently, more awareness is being raised about the negative effects of over-scheduling young children. Think of the old expression:

31

too many logs on the fire smothers the flames. Modern day psychologists and family counselors are speaking out on the dangers of children who feel stressed, anxious, and overworked. We all need time to rest and recharge. If someone never has a day off in their busy week, their family bonds and friendships will suffer. Instead of enjoying all of his many activities, perhaps this boy felt exhausted and overwhelmed, although he probably lacked the maturity or self-awareness to admit it. One wonders if conversations with his father centered only around reporting on his latest achievements rather than his thoughts, opinions, or feelings about life. Factor in the cultural aspect of stereotypical expectations for masculinity in the South, where "real men" did not admit to weakness or emotional vulnerability, and it is easy to see this teenaged boy as a tightly corked bottle ready to pop.

The book *Co-Dependency for Dummies* describes a high-achiever type of personality as someone with low self-esteem who tries harder and harder every day to be perfect in order to "earn" the right to be loved. Compulsion to over-achieve with a long list of accomplishments "is driven by internalized shame that they're flawed. An *A* student who obsesses over an *A-minus* on a test or that he missed a question is a perfectionist driven by shame.... Another example is a woman whose appearance must always be perfect. Even her home must be spotless. Her personal shame is projected onto her environment, which she sees as a reflection of her intolerable flawed self. Something chipped, dusty, or out of place can create painful anxiety, which she can stem only by fixing it rather than fixing her feelings about herself."

Of course it is impossible to psycho-analyze a person from a distance, and even more so, across the passage of time. These observations are based entirely on speculation and in no way are intended to blame his parents or his upbringing for what happened.

REGARDING MENTAL DEVELOPMENT from childhood to adolescence, the human brain continues maturing up to the age of mid-twenties, according to research done by the Juvenile Justice Center of the American Bar Association in 2004. In particular, the parts of the brain that govern impulsivity, risk-taking, common-sense judgment, planning for the future, and foresight of consequences are not fully developed in the brain of an adolescent.

M.R. Scism's article "Children are Different: The Need For Reform of Virginia's Juvenile Transfer Laws," published in 2019 in the *Richmond Public Interest Law Review* makes a solid argument for the idea that juveniles are ultimately less culpable than adults and should not face the same harsh consequences as adults. Scism's article cites a 2005 decision by the U.S. Supreme Court, in the case of *Roper v. Simmons*, where the court held that the death penalty was unconstitutional when applied to a person under the age of eighteen at the time of the crime. The court reviewed additional research supplied by the American Psychological Association on the developmental characteristics of late adolescents, featuring studies from a collection of experts in psychology, sociology, public policy, law and legal practice. They provided the court with expert opinions about the characteristics of adolescents such as less mature decision-making, impulsivity, risk-taking, peer orientation, temporal perspective (the extent to which long term and short term consequences are taken into account) and vulnerability to coercion and false confession. The research included MRI research on brain function suggesting that the brain continues to develop through young adulthood in areas that may bear on adolescent decision-making.

The court reached their conclusion and, in the published decision, summarized these three key differences between juveniles and adults: (1) lack of maturity and an underdeveloped sense of responsibility are found in youth more often than in adults and are more understandable among the young; (2) juveniles are more vulnerable or susceptible to negative influences and outside pressures, including peer pressure; (3) the character of a juvenile is not as well formed as that of an adult. The personality traits of juveniles are more transitory, less fixed. These qualities often result in impetuous and ill-considered actions and decisions.

The landmark decision (*Roper v. Simmons*) formed a basis for two more cases that came before the U.S. Supreme Court in the next few years. In all three decisions, the U.S. Supreme Court relied on expert opinion research and analysis to reach the same conclusion: that juveniles do not have the same developmental and cognitive abilities as adults. Therefore, the experts argue that juveniles are less culpable than adults and should not face the same harsh penalties that adults do. For these same reasons, almost every state prohibits those under age eighteen from voting, signing contracts, serving on juries, or getting married.

Scism's article clearly explains that adolescents are not yet the person they will ultimately become. Crimes committed in youth represent a temporary phase of experimentation in risky behavior. Usually, the acts of juvenile offenders are the product of immature judgement rather than an inherent "bad" character. The article makes a strong argument that transferring a juvenile to adult court and prison weakens a youth's chances at rehabilitation that would occur through the natural course of psychological development as they get older.

The hypothetical question can never be answered, whether that sixteen year old boy loitering in the Parish House kitchen on that night would have behaved the same way as the older version of himself. Would an eighteen or twenty-five year old Lee Scott have reacted with the same level of uncontrolled, impulsive rage in an argument with an outspoken young girl? Did this crime only happen because of his youth and immaturity?

Chapter 5. Extracting a Confession

BEFORE DESCRIBING THE events of that night when Lee Goode Scott killed Dana Marie Weaver, let's first examine the source of the narrative. Aside from the physical evidence at the scene, there is only one point of view. One person alone saw what unfolded on the evening that ended with a young girl dead on the floor. There were no eyewitnesses. From the moment Dana Marie waved good-bye to her friends and entered the Parish House of Christ Episcopal Church, whatever she may have said or done was reported to the police by none other than her killer.

The question is, can we truly know what really happened? Human memory can be a tricky thing. Memories in the mind of a sixteen-year old boy are even trickier.

When the police first brought Lee Scott in for questioning, he claimed to have no memory of his actions on that Sunday night. He insisted on a foggy recollection of where he had been during the hours of the attack. On the first day of his arrest, the police interrogated him for up to seven hours. They asked if he would like to see a picture of Dana. "No, I don't care to," he was quoted as saying. Even so, the crime scene photograph was placed before him. His expression did not change as he looked at the face of his victim. Newspapers remarked upon how "unemotional" the youth appeared to be.

The police assumed he was lying to evade scrutiny. But, was he actually telling the truth about having amnesia?

Short answer is yes.

Since the 1980s, a number of psychological studies have documented the claims of partial or total amnesia by offenders of violent crimes. The numbers range anywhere from ten to twenty percent of men charged with various crimes who have no memory, or partial memory, of the incident. This so-called "crime-related amnesia" occurs most frequently in murder or manslaughter cases but also sexual crimes or domestic violence. Excluding the obvious black-out effects of drugs or alcohol, as much as seventy percent of murder cases involve amnesia to some degree or another. Especially in crimes of passion committed in the heat of the moment, the killer may be the one most unable to face what happened.

Laws and courts are supposed to punish the guilty after fairly examining the evidence. The legal term *mens rea* refers to a person's mental state while committing an offense. In order to be guilty of a crime, other than negligence, the defendant must act voluntarily in carrying out the deed. That is, they must be knowingly aware of their behavior. They must purposefully intend to engage in an activity that produces a desired result. The U.S. Constitution, and penal codes at the federal and state level, are designed to protect the innocent from being unfairly accused. Although the justice system has often failed in practice, and thousands have been incarcerated or executed in error. Yet, our laws proclaim a lofty ideal of fairness and impartiality—the idea that Lady Justice is blind—that judges, prosecutors and defense attorneys work every day to uphold.

The basic concept of due process means a person must be competent to stand trial and understand the charges being held against them. What happens if a defendant cannot remember committing the offense for which they are accused? What if they are truly sincere in declaring innocence, when their own mind is shielding their conscience from the horror of their own crime?

Scholars have categorized two types of crime-related amnesia. *Organic amnesia* is caused by some sort of neurological defect such as paranoid schizophrenia. *Dissociative amnesia* is the failure to remember the events of a traumatic experience, even without a neurological defect. It is well known that stressful situations cause over-secretion of hormones that impair long-term memory recall. What could be more stressful than committing a homicide?

Amnesia is easy to fake. A suspect in an investigation only needs to say, "I don't remember." It is the rare criminal who admits guilt without hesitation. Generally, the courts do not recognize amnesia itself as a defense. Unlike the plea of insanity, which can be shown with a history of mental illness, the unique category of crime-related amnesia is often temporary and limited to the days or weeks following a specific crime. How can this type of amnesia be objectively proven? How can investigators separate the truth from the lies? Several testing methods are available: the polygraph, hypnosis, personality tests, and drugs.

FLOWERS FOR DANA: THE 1949 MURDER OF DANA MARIE WEAVER IN THE "STAR CITY" ROANOKE, VIRGINIA

Lee Scott underwent interrogations, on and off, for about eleven days at the Roanoke City jail within the Municipal Building downtown. Along with the detectives, the team included one or more psychiatrists to observe the teenager's mental state during questioning. There was some question of whether the suspect would be given a formal mental examination, or as the newspapers called it, a "sanity test." Journalists found an anonymous source within the police department who discussed (off the record) much of what the youth had admitted thus far.

Lee Scott told his story of going to Christ Episcopal Church about 5:30 PM intending to meet another friend who never arrived. Then Dana Marie entered at some time before 6:00 PM and surprised him. He stated that he did not have an appointment to meet with her. The two had never dated and were only casually acquainted as students attending the same high school.

What took place afterwards, he could not clearly recall. He experienced a black-out and a significant gap of time in his memory.

He recalled leaving the church premises about one hour later, although he could not say by which exit he emerged. For a while, he stood on the corner of Franklin Road and Washington Avenue looking up at the twilight sky. Then he went home, undressed, and got into bed. Restless and unable to sleep, he listened to music on the radio.

As described in more detail in the following chapters, Lee Scott walked to school on Monday morning as per his routine. On the way, his friend commented on the scabs of scratches on his face, and Lee blamed it on poison oak. When Dana Marie's killing appeared in the afternoon newspapers, he figured it was all a bad dream. Even he could not believe it himself that he could have done such a thing. Part of his mind built a wall to shield his consciousness from the awful truth.

One day later, an anonymous phone call to police led officers to the high school. Lee Scott was summoned to the principal's office and from there things proceeded quickly. His father Norman Garrett Scott allowed the detectives into his son's bedroom where they found clothing soiled with blood.

By Tuesday night, Lee Scott was under arrest and officially charged with murder. The detectives had circumstantial evidence but not a confession.

He was held in jail, without bond, all the while maintaining under interrogation that his memory was hazy. He did not recall doing harm to the girl. The days dragged on. Forensics laboratories at the FBI analyzed the blood found on the clothing stashed in his closet. All the while, "Buddy" insisted to his weeping mother's face that absolutely he did *not* commit the crime.

Newspapers printed a daily update for their readers hungry to know every detail. Looking back at the unfolding saga, it appears that the youth was not represented by an attorney when the police first brought him in for questioning.

Everyone who has watched a police drama on television knows the Miranda Warning by heart: "You have the right to remain silent. Anything you say can be used against you in court. You have the right to talk to a lawyer for advice before we ask you any questions. You have the right to have a lawyer with you during questioning. If you cannot afford a lawyer, one will be appointed for you before any questioning if you wish. If you decide to answer questions now without a lawyer present, you have the right to stop answering at any time."

The language used in this warning would be developed almost twenty years later, after a U.S. Supreme Court decision in 1966 known as *Miranda v. Arizona*. Although the precise language can vary, the basic idea is to protect an individual in custody from a violation of their Fifth Amendment right against compelled self-incrimination or Sixth Amendment right to counsel. The courts have since ruled that the warning must be meaningful. The suspect being arrested must be asked if they understand their rights and should respond "yes" or "no." Some jurisdictions require that a police officer ask "do you understand?" after every sentence in the warning. Evidence has in some cases been ruled inadmissible because of an arrestee's poor knowledge of English and the failure of arresting officers to provide the warning in the arrestee's language.

Did Lee Scott waive his right to have an attorney present during the early hours of questioning by police? Or, as a minor, did his parents make that decision for him? Until he was formally charged with a crime, did his parents not consider the idea that he needed an attorney by his side? The topic of juvenile Miranda Rights has been extensively debated in the last fifty years and is well beyond the scope of this book. It is enough to say that the Roanoke City police department in 1949 did not follow the same procedures as police officers might follow today.

The case passed quickly into the hands of Commonwealth Attorney for the City of Roanoke, Curtis Emery "C.E." Cuddy who had occupied the role for about seven years. As Virginia is technically called a commonwealth, not a state, this position is equivalent to a district attorney or a state attorney. Mr. Cuddy's duty was to prosecute all misdemeanors and felonies that occurred in the city of Roanoke and its suburbs. He brought cases to both the juvenile and adult courts. Mr. Cuddy was a man in his mid-forties, a family man and the father of two children.

C.E. Cuddy scheduled Lee Scott for a preliminary hearing in Juvenile Court for the week immediately following his arrest. Cuddy told reporters that if the court found sufficient evidence, he would be held for the next session of the Grand Jury just like any adult charged with murder.

Meanwhile, the sixteen-year-old was confined in the regular portion of the city jail. Every night, he was locked into a cell with three adult men. During the day, he had access to a common area corridor outside the cells, along with about thirty other prisoners being held at the time. The Scott family began to realize that their son was not coming home anytime soon. They retained the services of a defense attorney a few days after his arrest.

On May 21, after eleven days of going in circles around Lee Scott's denials and claims of amnesia, the police administered a dose of Sodium Pentothal with his parents' consent. Up until that day, his father maintained the hope of his son's innocence. Mr. Scott told reporters that he suspected his son of covering up and protecting someone else. In the face of overwhelming circumstantial evidence, he could not believe that his only son could commit such a brutal act. The righteous upstanding citizen desperately searched for an excuse to explain away the blood on his son's hands.

Truth serum is a misleading term for a variety of barbiturate drugs. The idea, in popular culture, is an injection which inhibits the ability of a subject under questioning to have presence of mind to lie. How many spy movies depict a glassy-eyed "bad guy" tied to a chair, under a bright light bulb, answering questions in an uninhibited monotone.

Many barbiturates fall under the truth serum category. One drug is Scopolamine, now infamous as a date-rape drug that causes retrograde amnesia, that is, the inability to recall events prior to its administration. Sodium Pentothal was commonly used in operating rooms as a general anesthesia but in recent years has been replaced by more effective alternatives. There are many others but all of the truth serum drugs work in the same manner. The effects are similar to consuming large amounts of alcohol. These drugs act to depress the central nervous system and interfere with judgment and higher cognitive function. A person under the influence of truth serum may regurgitate a free-flow of information which can be a blend of fact and fantasy with many details exaggerated, distorted, or omitted.

Such drugs had widespread use in the 1950s, especially by three-letter government agencies during the rampant paranoia of the Cold War era. Later, in the 1960s, the U.S. Supreme Court ruled that a confession produced under the influence of truth serum was unconstitutionally coerced. Subsequently, the use of such drugs declined as an interrogation tool.

But this was the spring of 1949, and the Roanoke City police department was running out of patience. They were frustrated at being unable to extract a confession. Delays upon delays came with waiting for forensics labs to analyze the physical evidence: Lee Scott's blood-stained clothing, the scrapings from under the girl's fingernails, and other items from the crime scene. All the while, the whole city buzzed with gossip and rumors. Outraged citizens clamored for justice.

Lee Scott's confession under the influence of truth serum was audio recorded by the police but never released to the public. A summary of his confession was revealed for the first time in his defense attorney's opening statement at trial. The confession on record was a hazy narrative coming out of a drug-induced mental fog that is a blended mixture of his memory, his fantasy, and his primal need for self-preservation. Whether his story is the whole truth of what happened in Dana Marie Weaver's final moments, only God knows.

Chapter 6. Losing Control in the Moment

POLICE RECORDED LEE Goode Scott's confession given under the influence of a truth serum drug, but the audio recording was filed away and never saw the light of day. The world had to wait until his defense attorney's opening remarks at trial to hear the story according to the one person who walked out of that kitchen alive. Here is what he confessed—what may or may not have actually happened.

The fateful Sunday of May 8, 1949 began with the routine of every other Sunday that came before. Lee Scott carefully combed his dark hair styled in a fashionable crewcut. He dressed in his best suit and tie for attending the morning worship services at Christ Episcopal Church.

Side by side with his parents and younger sister, he listened to Rev. Garrett's inspiring homily that spoke about the value of family. He stood confidently in the choir among the other clean-cut youths as they sang hymns to the lofty rafters of the chapel. As the reverend would later comment to the news-hungry journalists in the early days after the police made their arrest, "Everything we know about the boy is good. He has a clean reputation."

For some unexplained reason, Lee Scott did not join the Young People's Service League in their day-long excursion out of town. Instead, he chose to stay home. Perhaps he celebrated Mother's Day with a family luncheon.

In the afternoon, he made plans to meet a high school friend named Fred Bradley at Christ Episcopal Church's Parish House. He must have known about the youth group's out-of-town event and so he expected to have the recreational facilities all to himself. He looked forward to a boys' night out playing a few games of table tennis (a.k.a. ping-pong) before going out to the movies. The Frank Sinatra-Gene Kelly feature film *Take Me Out to the Ballgame* was playing at the American Theater in downtown Roanoke.

Lee Scott arrived at the Parish House a little after 5:30 PM, about fifteen or twenty minutes before Dana Marie Weaver was dropped off at the curb. He loitered alone in the empty building, watched the clock ticking, and waited for his friend to show. When he heard footsteps entering the building, he first thought it was Fred Bradley. How surprised he must have been to see another one of his schoolmates, a girl that he knew casually from passing in the hallways between classes. Also, they may have associated with each other at prior meetings of the Sunday youth group. They exchanged a polite "hello" and some light conversation before matters spiraled wildly out of control.

At first, Lee Scott still wanted to have a game of ping-pong. If his buddy had failed to show, then he resigned to make do with the girl. They looked about and could not find the equipment, however. The vacant building had little else to offer in the way of entertainment.

The two of them went upstairs to the kitchen to have soft drinks. Instead of the popular Coca-Cola, they chose a competitor product Dr. Pepper. They stood face-to-face while they sipped from six-ounce glass bottles of the sparkling dark beverage.

Their conversation turned sour when Dana Marie criticized Jimmy Webb, one of their fellow students at the high school.

Jimmy Webb was a star athlete at school who had recently won the state's wrestling championship. Indeed, the Virginia Wrestling Association (VAWA) website has lists going back to 1949 that show his name. The lists do not go back any further because the sport of wrestling in Virginia only got its start in the late 1930s and teams did not begin serious activity until after World War II. According to the 1949 yearbook of Jefferson High School, the wrestling squad under the guidance of Coach Nick Carter was in its second year of existence and growing in popularity. The yearbook showcases the activities of Jimmy Webb and his peers. The shirtless young men wearing Superman-style tight shorts and leggings are depicted in various positions grappling each other on the gym mats.

The 1949 state tournament, the first of its kind, was held at the University of Virginia in Charlottesville. Only five schools were qualified to send a total of about fifty wrestlers to compete. In the early days, Virginia held one and only one tournament for all schools both public and private. Beginning in 1970, the state tournament would be divided into three divisions for public schools and private schools developed their own separate league. But in 1949, in the earliest year that tournament winners are recorded, Jimmy Webb faced competitors from all over the state. His family and friends must have been very proud of him coming out on top in this brand-new sport, winning a trophy at something no Virginia high school student had ever won before.

Perhaps Lee Scott knew from the high school rumor mill that Webb was her former boyfriend. Or perhaps he had no idea why Dana Marie harbored some bitterness about her ex-boyfriend and spoke of him in unflattering terms. The couple had quarreled and broke up about one month before. In this context, it is understandable that Dana Marie played down Jimmy Webb's accomplishments. She told Lee Scott that Jimmy Webb was "no good" and that he won the state championship by sheer luck rather than athletic prowess.

On the witness stand during his murder trial, Lee Scott explained to the jury in his own words the conversation leading up to the moment when he snapped. "She said he drank too much, that he was just a drunkard. I told her not to talk about him like that. He was a nice boy. She said he wasn't any good. Just lowdown. He was just lucky that he won the wrestling championship."

What Dana Marie did not know—while sipping Dr. Pepper and trash-talking her ex-boyfriend—was that Lee Scott idolized Jimmy Webb to a nearly unhealthy degree. His defense attorney described to the jury a serious case of hero worship, saying in his opening remarks that his client "admired and worshipped" the high-school wrestler.

Her remarks triggered a burst of rage in the young man. Like a bowstring pulled to its limit and suddenly released, he snapped. In his own words spoken on the witness stand at the murder trial, "Something just swept over me and I hit her."

IN HIS BOOK *Why We Snap*, R. Douglas Fields PhD examines this human phenomenon of the seemingly irrational rage response from the widespread incidents of road rage to a variety of random outbursts—including Dr. Fields's own anecdote of seeing red while fighting a gang of pickpockets while on vacation in Barcelona. "No matter where you live, the daily papers and news media are filled with similar instances where 'normal' law-abiding individuals with no history of violence suddenly 'snap' and attack violently. Often the rage is triggered by the slightest provocation." (pp. 11-12) Dr. Fields explains the human brain's chemistry, structure, and functions to define what he calls a rage response circuit. When the right sort of environmental trigger flips the switch in certain areas of the brain, the acts of extreme violence or cruelty are not the results of insanity. He makes the case that these crimes of passion do not originate in conscious reasoning; there is no planning or scheming beforehand. While making it clear that his exploration of the rage response circuit does not excuse the crimes, his book's goal is to explore the question of how this subconscious neural circuitry evolved out of survival behaviors from our distant past. The rage circuits are prone to misfiring in the modern world, in response to environmental triggers or stressors that did not exist a million years ago. We are no longer in the Stone Age where our distant ancestors needed that sudden rush of fighting spirit to fend off predators such as cave bears, sabertoothed tigers, and each other.

Dr. Fields outlines nine categories of rage triggers in what he calls LIFEMORTS meaning life/death situations that arise in defense of:

1. Life and Limb, the actual fight to defend your life
2. Insult, a challenge to establish dominance in a social group
3. Family, the biological need to protect one's offspring or immediate family
4. Environment, a threat to one's territory, home, or natural resources
5. Mate, the competition for or possession of a mate with whom to breed offspring
6. Order, to enforce the rules of society upon which our species depends for survival
7. Resources, to protect access to food, money, or valuable property
8. Tribe, to defend one's own group with the same zeal as defending family
9. Stopped, to escape restraint and especially when it could lead to a threat to life/limb

Frequently, a situation may involve more than one of these triggers. The more of them that are involved, not surprisingly, increases the likelihood of a violent outburst. Let's look again at this moment frozen in time: the two teenagers holding soda bottles, having a conversation, facing each other.

Dana Marie's words could have triggered him in several areas. First, an insult to a personal hero is what leads to barroom brawls, family feuds, or gentlemanly duels-to-the-death in the romantic past. After all, it is why Aaron Burr and Alexander Hamilton faced each other with pistols at dawn.

Also, Lee Scott may have also felt triggered by a sense of Order in society, that women and girls were not allowed to freely speak their minds if they had strong or contrary opinions. This was 1949 when a woman's place was supposed to be confined to the home as a dutiful wife and mother. As a church-going boy, he must have heard this Bible phrase: "A woman should learn in quietness and full submission. I do not permit a woman to teach or to assume authority over a man; she must be quiet." (1 Tim. 2:11-15 NIV) Add to that a dormant sense of imposter syndrome from the over-achieving sixteen-year-old boy who cannot tolerate any criticism of publicly-earned accolades or awards for exposing his own inner sense of inadequacy—especially from a female voice.

Finally, there could be the issue of tribal loyalty if he identified himself and Jimmy Webb as members of a fellowship of male athletes; no girls were allowed in their locker room or their clubhouse.

Understanding where the human brain originated and evolved, from an animal vulnerable to predators who were faster and stronger, Dr. Fields's book explains how these nine triggers are hard-wired into our nature. In particular, an insult (loss of dominance) or an upset to the social order meant one had limited access to the basic needs of food or shelter. To be on the lower rungs of the social ladder in prehistoric days was truly a threat to one's basic survival.

Thus, a cocktail of rage triggers mixed in the immature mind of this sixteen year old boy. As Lee Scott explained to the jury who would decide whether or not he had earned a death sentence for his crime, "Something just swept over me and I hit her."

HE CLUBBED HER IN THE head with the soda pop bottle already in his hand. The glass cracked, slashed her forehead, and started her profusely bleeding.

Right there, he had the opportunity to stop. As blood trickled down the girl's forehead, he could have backed off. *Oh gosh... Gee whiz... I'm sorry...*

What did I do... Any of those responses could have deescalated the conflict. A swimming instructor and an Eagle Scout would know first aid. If only he had come to his senses, in that split second, the whole matter could have ended. Sadly the "what if..." never happened. Instead, a series of rage circuits were triggered in the teenaged boy's mind. He had already snapped to the point of no return.

Dana Marie's survival instincts kicked into gear. Sensing his aggressive stance, she had no choice but to fight back. She swung back at her attacker in self-defense, either with her fists or her own soda pop bottle... or both.

Lee Scott knew some wrestling techniques from watching his idol Jimmy Webb grapple with opponents on the mat. Adrenaline kicked him into action mode. In the ensuing struggle, they overturned chairs, broke stacks of dishes, and knocked over the large stainless-steel coffee urn. From the condition of the furniture and kitchen appliances, the fight had to have lasted for several minutes.

When he tackled her and pinned her to the floor, his energy focused on trying to restrain or control her. This triggered Dana Marie's own rage circuits in defense against being pinned down. She did not shrink away or surrender to her larger, stronger opponent.

The struggle to regain her freedom soon turned into a more serious in the hand-to-hand fight for her very life. Dana Marie kicked in defense. Her movements were restricted by the slender, calf-length skirt and underclothes that were fashionable at the time. She had no other options but to reach up and claw at his face. She broke almost every one of her fingernails digging into his cheeks and neck but to no avail. Most likely she used chunks of broken glass to slash at his face.

He would come away with a large, deep gash spanning from the corner of his eye down to his chin. But the harder she fought, the harder Lee Scott fought to subdue her.

At trial, the prosecution would insinuate that Lee Scott has attempted to rape her. The coroner found no clear evidence of a sexual assault. The prosecutors based this theory entirely on the fact that her corpse was found with the skirt pulled up to her waist. Although it cannot be discounted that he could have attempted a sexual assault and not left behind any physical evidence.

His confession under the influence of truth serum drugs is not infallible. He could have been lying, even to himself.

There is also the possibility that her skirt could have raised simply by the act of lifting her legs to kick and struggle. At that time, the popular fashion for girls' skirts was a slender fit with a hemline at mid-calf or close to the ankles. It is not possible to fully raise one's legs for kicking unless the close-fitting long skirt is hoisted up out of the way. The final position of the body and her clothing is not, in itself, conclusive evidence beyond a reasonable doubt. Yet there is no way to know for sure if he attempted rape or not, as we only have one person's account of what happened. Whatever happened during those critical minutes can never truly be known.

In cross-examination on the witness stand, he stuck to his story. "I never tried to take advantage of a girl like that."

The prosecutor shouted into his face, "Didn't Dana give her life in trying to avoid you?"

"She fought very hard, sir."

"Fighting your advancements?"

"Not my advancements." Lee Scott confessed in the courtroom that although he had choked her, his only intent was to prevent her from scratching his eyes out. Eerily, his remarks echo a common excuse heard from domestic abusers who provoke a violent situation and then claim self-defense when their partner/victim is pushed into fighting back. Over and over, he maintained that he never meant to cause her death. Nonetheless, he held onto her neck for several minutes until she stopped struggling. Whether he used his bare hands in a dangerous wrestling choke hold, or whether he held another object to smother her face, the reports are not specific.

After Dana Marie lay still, he went into a daze. He backed away from the horrifying scene on the floor. Apparently, he experienced a psychological black-out where his rational mind could not face what his hands had just done. Turning away, he left her battered body lying there on the floor. The time was close to 7:00 PM when Lee Scott stumbled down the stairs to the exit.

Instinct prompted him to grab a paper sack to carry away a couple of things, though he may have been barely aware of his actions. He removed two articles of evidence from the crime scene. One item was the six-ounce soda pop bottle soiled with his bloody fingerprints. Beverages are still sold in glass today so it is easy to imagine a clear or light green bottle with a few drops of Dr. Pepper at the bottom.

The other item, identified in the newspaper accounts as a "coffee urn bag," is an unfamiliar vintage kitchen tool that required a bit of sleuthing to identify. Coffee urns are stainless steel cylinders that can percolate anywhere from forty-five to one hundred cups. Larger size urns are used in commercial restaurant or hotel kitchens or in banquet facilities such as the dining hall in the Parish House of a church. A modern coffee urn's standard design includes a mesh basket made of easy-to-clean stainless steel that serves the similar function of a drip basket in a household-size coffee brewing machine.

Back in the late 1940s, the newspaper's readers all knew that a coffee urn bag was an accessory to those older styles of the commercial appliance. As early as 1918, the National Urn Bag Company boasted in *Simmons' Spice Mill* magazine of their New York factory producing unbleached coffee urn bags at a rate of twenty thousand per week. (The company also manufactured the now-familiar single-serve tea bags which have survived the test of time.) Coffee urns continued to use cloth filter bags through the Great Depression and up through the second world war. The U.S. Navy published training manuals during World War II for those preparing meals—and the vitally important hot coffee—for large groups of servicemen aboard ship.

The typical coffee urn bag was made of muslin (a type of lower quality cotton cloth) and hemmed to hold an aluminum ring. No dimensions are given but it appears that the bag was roughly the size of a knitted beanie cap. A metal ring supported the bag's hemmed upper edge and rested on the inner rim of the coffee urn. To make a batch of coffee, one simply scooped powdery grounds into the bag and activated the machine to produce boiling water. Once the water dripped through to the end result, the urn bag needed to removed and thoroughly washed. These cloth bags could be re-used until they became too stained and had to be replaced.

Coffee urn bags fell out of fashion in the 1950s, despite their decades of use, when consumers preferred the stainless steel mesh baskets. A full-page advertisement in the 1947 issue of *The Journal of the American Hospital Association* speaks to potential customers about their common frustrations. "Torn filter papers, rancid or sagging urn bags can spoil your entire batch of coffee. Tri-Saver urns eliminate these hazards because they eliminate urn bags and filter paper."

Why go into so much detail about a seemingly small detail here? Because the coroner's autopsy report found strange discolorations on Dana Marie's neck and chin. The doctor could not explain the dark stains and cloth fiber abrasions until after the recovery of the coffee urn bag as evidence. By the time of trial, the facts became clear that Lee Scott fled the crime scene with these two items in his hands—the materials that he had used in battering his classmate. He bludgeoned her in the head with the bottle. He smothered her face or choked her with the coffee urn bag. Everything else he left behind as a mess for the janitor to clean up.

AS DESCRIBED IN AN earlier chapter, Lee Scott walked outside into the twilight. He loitered on the street corner for a little while. What a sight he must have been: a five foot eleven inch tall athletic youth, standing on the sidewalk, his trousers and Oxford shoes spattered with blood.

Ironically, he missed being spotted by a matter of minutes. About 7:15 PM, the grandmother of one of the youths in the Young People's Service League came to Christ Episcopal Church concerned that the group had not returned home. Mrs. Davis went to the second floor corridor of the Parish House and used the telephone mounted on the wall. She called the parents of another youth and learned they were still away at the all-day picnic.

While making that phone call, if only this worried grandmother had looked down the corridor into the dining hall. Just a few yards away from the telephone, she would have seen broken dishes and overturned chairs. Instead, Mrs. Davis went downstairs and waited on the doorstep for the youth group to return.

At first, Lee Scott headed for Fred Bradley's home about two blocks away from the church. During that short walk, the fog of his mind slowly began to clear. He realized that his clothes were covered in blood that was a mixture of another's and his own. As he put it, he was "all messy." He changed his mind about approaching the door or even tapping on a bedroom window. Instead, he ducked into the tree-shaded alleyway between his friend's house and the next-door neighbor. In the residential areas of Roanoke, Virginia, no fences separate one property from another. Only green grass, hedges or flowers mark the boundaries between homes. There in the shrubbery, he discarded the paper sack that contained the soda bottle and coffee urn bag as incriminating evidence.

He walked the rest of the way home and somehow avoided the close attention of his parents. They did not see him enter or tiptoe upstairs to his bedroom. He washed his hands. He dabbed at the deep bleeding gash on his cheek. He changed into clean clothes and stuffed the blood-stained clothing into the back of his closet.

Lee Scott ended his day by listening to the radio for a while. The bundle of bloodied clothing in the back of his closet soon faded from his thoughts. Like the Oscar Wilde story *The Picture of Dorian Gray*, the true image of his criminal act was contained elsewhere and apart from himself. "Upon the walls of the lonely locked room where he had spent so much of his boyhood, he had hung with his own hands the terrible portrait whose changing features showed him the real degradation of his life, and in front of it had draped the purple-and-gold pall as a curtain. For weeks he would not go there, would forget the hideous painted thing, and get back his light heart, his wonderful joyousness, his passionate absorption in mere existence. Then, suddenly, some night he would creep out of the house... he would sit in front of the picture, sometimes loathing it and himself, but filled, at other times, with that pride of individualism that is half the fascination of sin, and smiling, with secret pleasure, at the misshapen shadow that had to bear the burden that should have been his own.... Yet he was afraid... What if it should be stolen? The mere thought made him cold with horror. Surely the world would know his secret then. Perhaps the world already suspected it."

Pulling the covers up over his head, he went to sleep telling himself that it was all a bad dream.

Chapter 7. Hearing the News

"OUR MIDSTREAM STATUS in high school, arrived at in our junior year, is really an important stage. We have lost the bewilderment of sophomores and have a senior year to anticipate. Early in the year, we begin to take a real interest in the life at Jefferson. The strangers of last year are now our cherished teammates. We begin to walk together in many projects: student government, committee work of all kinds, athletic and literary contests, dramatics, spring carnival, hosts for the Junior-Senior prom. For several weeks the bustle of planning for this big event starts. Then there is the night of gaiety, fun, laughter, with the work and ideas of many a junior packed into our evening. Now at the close of our junior year, we are looking forward to that most glamorous of all years—our senior year." From *The Acorn*, Jefferson High School Yearbook of 1949.

Jefferson High School operated for fifty years educating the youths of Roanoke who were on the verge of adulthood. Originally constructed in 1922, the school opened its doors to a thousand students two years later. The first senior class graduated in 1925 and served the community until it shut down in the 1970s. The impressive red brick building is three stories high and over one hundred thousand square feet. It occupies most of a city block close to the center of town, in between Luck Avenue and Campbell Avenue SW, with Sixth Street SW as a border on the west.

In its prime, the bottom floor of the school held mostly vocational classes. The second floor contained the academic classrooms, the principal's office and the main office, gymnasium and entrance vestibule. The library, balcony, and scientific (chemistry and physics) laboratories were located on the third floor. The second-floor auditorium was modeled after a popular 17th century "shoe box" English opera house design, with a grand balcony, cushioned seats, and outstanding acoustics. Because the city had no civic center at the time, the auditorium was built for larger purposes than school dances. The space was used for community events and concerts, and in its day hosted such notables as internationally acclaimed symphony conductor Leonard Bernstein.

After the school closed in 1979, the vacant building became deteriorated. By the late 1980s, only pigeons and vandals soiled the halls that once bustled with teenagers hurrying to class. The Roanoke City Council appointed a citizens' committee, mostly of Jefferson High alumni, to determine the future of the iconic building. The inspiring story of the building's renovation and transformation is told on the website of what is now the Jefferson Center with Shaftman Performance Hall and multipurpose cultural community center. Today, the center is home base to nonprofit organizations involved in the performing arts, education and social services. The Jefferson Center Foundation, established in 1989, was spearheaded by the late Judge Beverly T. Fitzpatrick Sr. who was a 1939 graduate of Jefferson High School and ironically one of the team of prosecutors at Lee Scott's murder trial.

Looking back to that Monday morning of May 9, 1949, the prestigious high school became ground zero for events that would rock the city for decades to come.

AT BREAKFAST, LEE SCOTT'S parents observed nothing unusual in their son's behavior. They noticed the scratches on his face, and he lied saying either that it was pimples or that his after-school sports activities at the YMCA got a little rough. (The various newspapers are inconsistent in reporting on this detail.) Apparently, his mother tended to him with some ointment. One has to wonder if Mrs. Scott suspected her son of being untruthful, with a combination of her training as a nurse and a mother's experience of bandaging an active boy's scraped elbows and skinned knees.

Lee Scott showed up for classes on Monday morning as if nothing had happened the night before. He behaved the same as on any other day, calm and friendly, well-groomed and cleanly dressed. As the elected President of his Home Room (the first class of the day), he went through the motions of the daily routine: assisting the teacher with taking attendance, reciting aloud the principal's announcements, and leading his fellow students in the Pledge of Allegiance.

FLOWERS FOR DANA: THE 1949 MURDER OF DANA MARIE WEAVER IN THE "STAR CITY" ROANOKE, VIRGINIA

Classmates noticed the scab of a bloody gash along his right cheek. He coolly lied claiming to have scratched at poison oak. Not everyone was convinced of his excuse, but in the first few hours of the school day, no one had any reason to think of anything nefarious.

What the students did not know—as they moved from class to class, up and down the broad stairways inside the building—was that police detectives were examining the crime scene at a church less than a mile away. Before the days of social media and instant news, a couple of hours passed while the police notified the victim's mother and began their investigation. Journalists got wind of police activity but they had no live "breaking news" alerts.

In those days, events that required urgent attention were announced mostly on the radio. During World War II, the journalistic style of vivid "on the spot" reporting was dominated by the voice of Edward R. Murrow excitedly describing for his listeners what he witnessed. Movie theaters showed what are known as "newsreels" that recorded historic events on 35mm film shown on the big screen just before the main feature. When television networks came along, they required a new and different technology infrastructure and specialized broadcast towers spread slowly outside of the major cities like New York, Los Angeles, and Chicago. For a household in the late 1940s, a television set was more expensive, larger and bulkier than a radio. In 1949, less than one percent of households owned a television. The *CBS Evening News* premiered in April 1948 as a fledgling, experimental venture. Early news programs followed the narrative format of print newspapers. They generally believed that viewers got their news from local papers and radio stations; television stations saw little need to duplicate their efforts.

Newspapers commonly printed two editions per day—the morning and the evening. Occasionally, an extra edition would be printed in the afternoon for special breaking news that could not wait for the evening paper to roll "hot" off the printing presses. You may see newspaper delivery boys in old movies crying out, "Extra, extra, read all about it!" *The Roanoke Times* was the dominant local paper that tried to keep up with the latest happenings. Even so, gossip and word-of-mouth was how news travelled most quickly.

Dana Marie's teachers and friends may have wondered why she did not show up for school that day. Attendance-takers marked her "absent." Friends shrugged off their worries and planned to telephone her at home that evening.

Police tried to be discreet. By midday on Monday, they retraced the victim's steps according to the recollections of her distraught mother. When they reached out to ask Dana Marie's friends, "when was the last time you saw her alive?" the shocking news hit the student body. Faster than any social media posting, the verbal cries of students at Jefferson High School echoed through the hallways. So many were stunned and horrified. Dana Marie's friends asked to be excused from classes for the rest of the day.

Lee Scott finished out his classes, still keeping up the appearance of a normal routine. After the three o'clock bell, he walked a few blocks to the YMCA where he held a part-time after-school job as a swimming instructor. The eighteen-year-old supervisor Durwood Owens recalled looking at the afternoon edition of the newspaper along with a group of boys at the YMCA. They were in the middle of discussing the story of Dana Marie's murder when Lee Scott walked into the conversation. Nothing in his behavior seemed unusual, although Owens described the youth as easy-going, the perfect type to be a poker player, and the kind of person who never revealed his emotions. How true a characterization. Except for the scratches on his face, Lee Scott showed no outward signs of anything being amiss. He carried on with performing his duties as a swimming instructor for the full duration of his shift and left to go home for six o'clock supper.

Imagine the awkward conversation over the Scott's dinner table that evening. His father's voice likely dominated the room with expressions of righteous outrage. *Who could have done such an awful thing to an innocent girl? When the police catch this fiend, he should get the death penalty!* All the while, his son quietly ate his mother's cooking. He must have followed his everyday routine and excused himself to go up to his room. A few hours passed with the welcome distraction of homework studies. Lee Scott went to bed that night with the soiled bundle of clothing still hidden in the back of his closet. The tell-tale sack of crime scene evidence remained stashed in the bushes behind his friend's home a few blocks away. He closed his eyes and sank into the comforting dreams of denial.

Tuesday morning's edition of *The Roanoke Times* newspaper printed a front-page banner: "Jefferson High Girl Slain in Kitchen of Church." But this was hardly a local matter anymore. Newspapers outside of Virginia picked up the sensational story. The *Evening Star* in Washington D.C. called out in bold type: "Police Hunt for Clues in Church Slaying of Girl, 16, at Roanoke." Just underneath that headline, the words "Prowler is Suspected; Man with Scratched Face Being Sought" broadcast the only clue that the police detectives had to go on. Dana Marie had someone's blood and skin under her fingernails. The question was, who?

Lee Scott again showed up for classes on Tuesday morning as just another ordinary day. As the elected president of Home Room, his duty was to stand up in front of the class and read an announcement from the principal. His calm and steady voice asked his classmates for contributions on behalf of the victim's family. The money would be used to buy flowers for Dana Marie's funeral.

Everyone else was quivering with shock and choking back the urge to weep. Lee Scott matter-of-factly circulated through the room for collecting whatever cash or small change the students happened to be carrying.

Someone commented upon the scratches on his face and arms. The gashes and scrapes were still severe enough to be noticeable. One student remarked that Lee Scott might be the culprit. To which he responded, "Yeah, I killed her. Call the police." Not only did his joke fall flat but it started his grieving classmates whispering amongst themselves.

His cold demeanor and tasteless joke raised hackles. A few may have given him the benefit of doubt. After all, everyone deals with tragedy in different ways. But this group of teenagers had personal experience with grief; they had seen their parents and friends weep over the loss of loved ones during World War II; they had been pre-teens and early adolescents by the end of the war; the horror of death and one's reactions to it were well known. Gut instincts rippled through the student body. More than one person had a strong feeling that something was "off" about their classmate's battered appearance and unemotional behavior.

One person made the courageous, agonizing decision to take action. A young woman trusted her instincts and listened to her inner voice whispering fears. She may have hesitated to cast suspicion on a classmate but could not ignore that gnawing feeling in her gut that something was not right. Her name was kept anonymous for a while. Later the newspapers revealed her identity when she collected the cash reward for giving police the break they were praying for.

About noon on Tuesday, the police department received a telephone call from Beverly Francis Barnes—a senior at Jefferson High and a member of the cheerleader squad. Miss Barnes had been among the mixed group of high school and college students who enjoyed a Sunday afternoon socializing with Dana Marie Weaver in the hours before her death. No accusation was made by the young girl on the phone, just a suggestion that Lee Scott might have some knowledge of the crime.

With no other suspects and little else to guide their investigation, the detectives went over to the school. They did not wish to alarm the other students. Detective Captain Webb notified William D. Payne, the high school's principal.

Together they came up with a plan to request Lee Scott come to the principal's office on an errand. Once the youth arrived, the detectives saw the scratches on his neck and the deep gash cut into his face. Poison oak or pimples was a pathetic excuse that the police did not believe for one moment. They asked if he would accompany them to police headquarters to answer some questions. Without objection, the boy calmly agreed. Obedient to the point of being docile, he put up no struggle. They escorted him out a back door and into their car for the short drive to the detective's office.

After some time, Lee Scott's father was alerted. Mr. Garrett Scott left work and drove to the police headquarters. Stunned by the accusation against his son, eager to prove his innocence, he invited the detectives to his own home. No search warrant was needed. I imagine that Mr. Scott challenged the policemen, go ahead, search my son's room, you won't find anything here. How wrong he was. There, in the youth's bedroom closet they discovered a stash of dirty laundry: a corduroy coat, trousers, and a pair of tan-and-white Oxford shoes. All of the clothing showed what appeared to be blood stains. I can only wonder how many times Mr. Scott must have said the word "no" on that day. He shook his head and blinked his eyes in denial of the evidence that the policeman's hands brought out into the light.

Around the same time as the police discovered the bloody clothing in the youth's bedroom closet, another team of officers went to search the bushes in the grassy alleyway by a house not far from the church. Lee Scott had told them where to find a discarded paper sack containing a soda pop bottle and a coffee urn bag with blood stains.

Students from the high school gathered in the first floor corridor of the Municipal Building downtown. They watched the detectives and Mr. Scott coming and going with satchels in hand. No comments were made to the public all afternoon. More and more spectators continued to arrive as the sky darkened into the late hours of Tuesday evening. Finally, about 9:30 PM, Detective Captain Webb held a press conference to announce that Lee Goode Scott would be formally charged with the murder of Dana Marie Weaver.

Every parent locked their doors and pulled their curtains tight. Every teenaged girl stayed home. Dana Marie's father Murrell Weaver drove into town from nearby Lynchburg to offer comfort to his ex-wife and his only surviving child. The Weavers grieved for the loss of their daughter taken so suddenly and unexpectedly. But they were not the only family to weep that night. The Scott family had their world turned upside down as well. Nothing would ever be the same.

THE FUNERAL FOR DANA Marie Weaver on Wednesday consumed the entire town. Jefferson High School dismissed classes at 2:00 PM but a crowd had already begun to gather when her body was transported from the funeral home to the Raleigh Court United Methodist Church. Dana Marie's father Murrell F. Weaver arrived at the church alone and took a seat several minutes before his ex-wife entered. The grieving mother was supported by Richard Weaver, her twenty-three-year-old son and only surviving child. When the services began at 4:00 PM, hundreds of attendees filled the church and spilled out into the streets. Florists ran out of flowers; the Oakey Funeral Home required two trucks to deliver all of the flowers.

The Rev. William Watkins provided a simple funeral service of prayer and the Methodist funeral liturgy. There was no sermon. The reverend read from the Bible the well-known verses of the 23rd Psalm: "*The Lord is my shepherd; I shall not want. He maketh me to lie down in green pastures: he leadeth me beside the still waters. He restoreth my soul: he leadeth me in the paths of righteousness for his name's sake. Yea, though I walk through the valley of the shadow of death, I will fear no evil: for thou art with me; thy rod and thy staff they comfort me. Thou preparest a table before me in the presence of mine enemies: thou anointest my head with oil; my cup runneth over. Surely goodness and mercy shall follow me all the days of my life: and I will dwell in the house of the Lord for ever."*

The all-white casket remained closed for the service. Floral wreaths banked around the casket, across the front and sides of the church. A large cross formed of white gardenias was placed above the choir which stood several feet back of the casket. On the casket itself was a spray of salmon-colored gladioli, white carnations, white lilies, and pink roses. The choir sang hymns of "Nearer My God to Thee" and "Abide With Me" that those attendees who were not choked with weeping joined in singing.

The hearse left the church and carried Dana Marie's casket to Evergreen Cemetery to be buried near her brother killed in action in World War II. The services at the grave were brief. Most of the hundreds who gathered to pay their respects remained standing until the casket was lowered into the ground.

On that day, it seemed the whole city of Roanoke turned out into the streets to grieve. For those who barely knew her—or not at all—on that day, Dana Marie became everyone's daughter, everyone's sister, everyone's best friend.

Chapter 8. Finding the Culprit

LOOKING BACK TO WHEN the church's rector Rev. Garrett made the phone call to report what the custodian had found, Roanoke City's police officers H.L. Britt and C.E. Shelor were the first responders on the scene. Police involvement began on Monday morning, May 9, 1949 at some time before 10:00 AM.

Officers Britt and Shelor stood side-by-side with Rev. Garrett on the second floor kitchen of the Parish House and made their first examination of the body lying in a pool of blood on the floor. Even for hardened policemen used to dealing with robberies, assaults, and domestic violence calls, the sight of a teenage girl's body on the floor of a church kitchen must have chilled their souls to the core.

The usual procedural steps were taken to document the evidence at the crime scene. Tempers must have flared with a sense of urgency to find the monstrous brute who could have committed such an outrageous act. A police photographer arrived to snapshot the position of the victim's body and the objects all around. Forensics teams sprinkled a fine powder on surfaces likely to hold fingerprints, brushed away the excess, and used cellophane tape to "lift" images. Others collected the victim's personal effects, such as pocketbook and wristwatch, and made ready to transport the body to the coroner's office.

The city coroner Dr. Charles M. Irvin examined the corpse and performed an autopsy. He removed bits of someone's skin from underneath Dana Marie's broken fingernails, indicating that she had scratched the face and arms of her attacker in a desperate struggle for her life. He reported a large bruise on her neck, and other bruises on her legs, but no obvious evidence of being raped. Cause of death was determined to be "asphyxia by choking" and not the blow to her head or loss of blood. Dr. Irvin delayed signing her death certificate for a few days until the laboratory results came back to confirm his initial assessment. He ruled her death a homicide.

Police searched the immediate area around the church for any suspicious persons, even though twelve hours had gone by and the perpetrator was certainly long gone. There had been previous complaints of attempted assaults in the area. The church had twice been ransacked in recent months. Ironically the police recently had increased patrols in the neighborhood. On Monday afternoon, they detained an unnamed person who, oddly, was changing his shirt while sitting inside his automobile. This person was thoroughly questioned and released; his name was never mentioned in the newspapers.

Detective Captain Frank H. Webb took control of the investigation in partnership with Commonwealth Attorney C.E. Cuddy. The two men wasted no time in spending the rest of Monday interviewing the list of persons who had last seen the girl alive. Everyone they spoke with had an air-tight alibi for their whereabouts the day before—from the janitor Alexander Roland who found the body to the college students who dropped her at the curbside. The VPI students verified arrival at their dormitories on campus.

Mr. Roland had been out of town all weekend. It bears mentioning that he may have carried the latest edition of the "Negro Motorist Green Book" that provided a directory of hotels and other establishments that were considered to be safe ports of call for African American travelers. The Jim Crow policies of "whites only" limited the availability of food and lodging services for black travelers. First published in 1936, the Green Book was the inspiration of a New York postal carrier named Victor Hugo Green who had grown weary of the discrimination against those who dared to venture outside of their designated neighborhoods. Reportedly, Mr. Roland safely returned home to Roanoke late in the evening and well after the girl's estimated time of death.

The detective's initial theory was that Dana Marie had gone to the Parish House expecting to attend a meeting of the Young Peoples League. As she had spent the day earlier with friends not associated with the church, she did not know that the group had changed plans and instead went for an excursion out of town. Police speculated that the girl went upstairs to use the telephone mounted on the wall in the corridor near the kitchen. She may have surprised a prowler who then attacked her.

Captain Webb mailed the fingernail-scrapings, the fingerprint images, and other physical evidence to an FBI forensics lab in Washington D.C. He held out little hope of useful clues coming from laboratory scientists peering into microscopes or fingerprint analysts squinting into magnifying glasses. He had never heard of DNA evidence; in 1949, no one ever had. The discovery of the double helix DNA structure was announced in 1953 but it would not become an effective tool for criminal investigations until years later. At the time of Captain Webb investigating Dana Marie's murder, he could only hope to learn the blood type of the attacker, whether it was a male or female, and little else. Even if they could get legible fingerprints, that kitchen was used by countless people all day long. Dozens and dozens of hands had touched everything in the room twice over.

At forty-seven years old, Captain Webb was an experienced police detective who rose up the ranks in the usual ways. The City of Roanoke's website displays an illustrated history of their police department. He served under Police Chief S.A. Bruce and, as captain of the detective bureau, Captain Webb was next in line to become police chief himself in 1952. He is mentioned in various newspaper accounts for responding to a number of crimes over the years such as a string of armed robberies and vicious assaults. None of those cases perplexed him like this one did in its early hours.

A slender, stern-looking, gray-haired man with wire-rimmed glasses, Captain Webb took on the burden of trying to solve the city's most notorious murder of the 20th century. As the daylight faded and night began to fall, he slumped over his desk. Looking at the black-and-white photographs of the girl's battered corpse, he wondered who could have done such a thing.

Captain Webb told reporters clamoring for something to print in Monday's evening edition, "We are just grabbing at straws."

His imagination and fledgling efforts at criminal profiling fell far short of reality. In our modern day, we are well acquainted with the likes of Ted Bundy and Jeffrey Dahmer the serial killers who walked openly under the guise of being ordinary. However, at the time of Dana Marie's murder, another sensational case to capture national attention was the so-called Black Dahlia, the nickname for a young woman found mutilated in Los Angeles in January 1947 just two years earlier. That killer was never caught.

How many times have we heard the expression, so-and-so doesn't "look" like a murderer. The stereotype is deeply ingrained in our psyche, the idea that we should be able to spot a predator—a killer—in our midst. Just as a flock of sheep knows to run away from a snarling wolf, and gazelles will stampede to escape a hungry lion, we humans crave the illusion of security by assuming we know when to stay or when to flee.

In the Victorian Era, a concept called criminal anthropology was a widespread theory that detectives used for profiling and identifying suspects of violent crime. As described in Christer Holmgren's book *Cutting Point*, the London police may have overlooked a likely suspect for the Jack the Ripper murders because a certain innocuous-looking fellow, found standing near the freshly-fallen body of a bleeding victim, was assumed to be a witness or an innocent passer-by. Criminologists in the previous century spent their efforts in examining the physical characteristics of murderers, measuring their skulls, comparing the thickness of their foreheads, and other such tell-tale signs of sub-human characteristics. The idea was that criminality could be linked to vestiges of an older genetic heritage that lacked civilized attributes. A criminal's natural disposition to commit acts of evil was expected to be observable in their physical traits. An Italian physician named Cesare Lombroso was the father of such ideas, the belief that criminality had its cause in biological properties. He promoted his idea of cultural anthropology, of biological degeneration as a cause for criminality. Psychiatrists and philosophers of the Victorian Era assumed that humanity will always develop on a line of positive evolution. According to this idea, civilization's forward-moving development should ultimately lead to each new generation being more refined than the last. The logical extension of this idea would be that things like war and violent crime would dissolve over time and we would set course toward an ideal society. However, no one can deny that such things as war, genocide, violence and cruelty continue to exist even after tens of thousands of years. Victorian criminologists explained away this paradox with the idea that mankind's long-lost primitive urges, a residue of our primordial ancestors, could spontaneously reemerge after several generations.

These stereotypes persisted into America's popular culture of the 1930s and 1940s. Hollywood pumped out too many low-budget, black-and-white gangster movies to count. The pulp fiction detective magazines featured tawdry cover art, usually with a damsel in distress and the shadowy, distorted sneer of evil-doers lurking in the shadows. Heroes wore the white hats.

Roanoke's police detectives were looking for a prowler, a vagrant, a grown man with a brutish soul who was loose rampaging on the streets. They assumed that such a horrific, violent killing could have only been performed by someone with a history of assault. They held a false idea that such crimes were committed only by certain types of people in certain "bad" neighborhoods. Surely, they thought, such a person would be easily identified by their disfigured appearance and savage behavior.

No one ever thought to look for murder suspects among the clean, well-dressed students attending classes at Jefferson High School.

City Manager Arthur S. Owens offered a $500 reward to anyone with information that would lead to the capture and arrest of Dana Marie's killer. He went to bed Monday night praying for someone—anyone—to come forward with a clue. Little did he know how quickly the mystery would be solved. Within twenty-four hours, an anonymous tip would lead detectives to Jefferson High School and by Tuesday night, they would have the culprit in custody.

Chapter 9. Defending the Accused Killer

ON WEDNESDAY MORNING, May 11, 1949, Mr. Garrett Scott picked up the telephone in search of an attorney to help defend his son from the charges levelled against him. Mr. Scott clung to hope of his son's total innocence. He held onto the elusive fantasy that someone else committed the horrific deed and his son was gallantly lying to protect a fiendish friend's identity. "Maybe he came in and found somebody attacking her," Mr. Scott told reporters. "He told me he didn't know what happened. All he knew was that he had blood on his hands."

Lee Scott's frail mother shared her husband's belief in their son's innocence. Mrs. Scott baked cookies and brought him a Sunday-best tweed suit to be photographed by a bustling crowd of journalists. She revealed to reporters a conversation that she held with her boy locked in the jailhouse. "Buddy, you couldn't?" she asked, to which he replied, "No, mother, of course not."

Within forty-eight hours, Mr. Scott found a lawyer willing to take the case. The newspapers made note of this development on the following Friday—ironically, a Friday the 13th—that his parents secured the services of a prominent, well-known local defense attorney.

Mr. Thomas Warren Messick was forty-nine years old, married for about twenty-five years, and the father of several children including a teenaged son roughly the same age as the boy he would come to defend. Messick had a well-established career in Roanoke as a trial lawyer. During the era of Prohibition (that spanned from 1920 to 1933 when a U.S. Constitutional amendment prohibited the import, production, transport, or sale of alcoholic beverages), Messick had defended many an outlaw when Roanoke and the surrounding rural counties were hotbeds of "moonshiners" and bootleggers violating the prohibition on alcohol. During World War II, Messick defended the manager of a retail store selling peanuts in downtown Roanoke. The store operated on Sundays, violating the so-called "blue laws" that strictly enforced the Christian idea of the "Lord's Day" being a day of rest; only businesses that provided necessities or conducted charitable works were exempt.

His most famous case was in 1927, when he filed a civil action against the Ringling Brothers Circus on behalf of two African-American albino brothers known by their circus sideshow stage names of Eko and Iko. Their mother, Harriet Muse, a native of Roanoke, accused the circus of abducting her young boys. As albinos, they were masqueraded as sideshow "freaks" and for years she had believed they were lost or dead. When the circus happened to come to Roanoke, she saw their pictures on an advertisement and bought a ticket to enter the tent where they were performing. Agents of the circus tried to pull the boys (now grown men) out of their mother's arms. Enter the attorney Warren Messick who fought the fast-talking show business lawyers and negotiated a settlement. The Muse brothers eventually returned to their show business career but with legitimate contracts, no longer as abductees being hidden from their family. In the end, they retired to Roanoke to quietly live out their days.

Messick earned the nickname "Squeak" because of his high-pitched voice. Beth Macy's book *Truevine* contains a detailed profile of the attorney's background based on personal interviews with Messick's law partner and with his son. His lilting accent was that of a central Virginia gentleman from growing up as the son of a farm manager in the Shenandoah Valley hills. His style of speech was punctuated by a rhythmic, repetitive flair. "Usually he would start his presentations with an appropriate story or joke that endeared him to his jury right away," according to his son who characterized his oral delivery "smooth as silk." Messick presented himself in court with a disheveled appearance. Unlike all other attorneys who wore formal dark suits in court, Messick dressed in casual sport jackets. "He looked like he was going out for a party," according to his junior law partner Harvey Lutins, whose nickname was Little Squeak for a while. "Only Mr. Messick could do that and get away with it."

Time and again, he proved to be a master at reaching into the hearts of a jury. He was known for shedding tears in his passionate oratories. Trials with Messick as defense lawyer became a spectator sport in Roanoke; workers often left their downtown offices early for the day to go watch his oratorial antics.

Messick was not afraid to take on a controversial case, as he had done many times before in his career. In those early days of Lee Scott's arrest, the newspapers and the gossip on the streets called for the head of Dana Marie's killer. He accepted the case, as any ethical defense lawyer would do—not so much for the sake of the Jefferson High School student locked up in the city jail, or even to condone the crime that was done, but for the ideals of the rule of law. The Fifth Amendment of the U.S. Constitution says to the federal government that no one shall be "deprived of life, liberty or property without due process of law." The townsfolk of Roanoke must have felt stunned and outraged at Messick for taking on the youth's defense. Phrases like "due process" and "innocent until proven guilty" must have rung hollow to the grieving family of the murdered girl.

Money did not motivate him, although Mr. Garrett Scott had enough of it to hire the best. Neither was Messick a civil rights crusader. He was simply pragmatic and had no political party affiliation, according to his partner Lutins. On one occasion in the late 1950s, while examining an African-American witness on the stand, Lutins as co-counsel addressed her as Mrs. Smith rather than by her first name. The judge was so outraged that he adjourned for recess to summon Lutins and Messick into chambers. As the story goes, the judge scolded them both. "Mr. Messick, you did not tell your young associate how we examine colored people here in my court." Messick deferred to the judge and matter-of-factly instructed his junior partner to never again call the witness Mrs. Smith. The trial reconvened and Lutins made sure to address the witness only as Mary. "That's the way it was," Lutins said. "Colored folk were not entitled to the dignity. Women weren't permitted to sit on juries. It was a different world back then."

It is a frequently asked question: how can a lawyer defend someone who is guilty of a horrible crime? The *Guardian* in 2014 published interviews of several attorneys who handled high-profile murder cases in "Defending the indefensible? Lawyers on representing clients accused of nightmarish crimes" and the effect it had on their personal lives. The attorney John Henry Browne spoke about his feelings when defending serial killer Ted Bundy. "The work is hard to shake off. You start looking at the world through dirty windows. I've been married a number of times and that partly has to do with my job. Living with me is very difficult. I do a lot of yoga and meditation. I'm really good at convincing myself I've compartmentalized all this stuff." Another attorney, William Kelley from California, defended Charles Ng who was convicted of torturing and murdering eleven people together with his accomplice Leonard Lake. "I don't get emotionally involved with my clients. I made that mistake once and it wiped me out. I guess I'm pretty mercenary. Just bring 'em on and I'll defend them. It makes you a better lawyer.... Was I horrified by my client? In the murder arena, you just don't have that sort of mindset. You're thinking, I'm going to do the darndest I can to defend this person as well as I possibly can. You want to prevail. You're battling the other side. Whether or not he gets off is up to the jury."

Messick visited the Roanoke City Jail in the Municipal Building for the first time to meet his teenaged client on Friday the 13th. Perhaps he thought of his own children who were roughly the same age. The boy's guilt or innocence did not enter his mind. His goal was to uphold the rule of law and provide a legal defense to the best of his ability.

As discussed in Chapter 5, Messick and Lee Scott's parents agreed to allow the police to administer truth serum a week later, on Saturday May 21, 1949, and to conduct an interrogation under the influence of the drugs. Up until that day, Mr. and Mrs. Scott desperately believed that their son was lying to shield the identity of someone else who was the real killer. Their hopes crashed to the ground in that hour, in that small gray room. As the reels of a tape recorder turned, the sixteen-year-old confessed to everything—the argument, the struggle, and his clumsy attempts at disposing of evidence.

Commonwealth Attorney C.E. Cuddy pushed for an early hearing of Juvenile Court as the first hurdle to overcome. A decision in Juvenile Court was needed to waive the process of trying the boy as a juvenile and moving Lee Scott up to adult court. Cuddy wanted to submit the case for the Hustings Court grand jury that was scheduled to convene its next session on June 6.

The whole idea of a Juvenile Court was relatively new. Before the 20th century, juveniles were treated no differently than adults accused of crimes. With the era of industrialization came the idea of *parens patriae* (Latin for "parent of the nation") that refers to the public policy power of the state to intervene against a child's parent or legal guardian. The state can assume the role of parent to any child in need of protection. The Juvenile Court system which developed in the early 1900s was very different from adult court by having more informal and closed proceedings that resembled civil law, with emphasis on helping the child, and absence of jury trials.

FLOWERS FOR DANA: THE 1949 MURDER OF DANA MARIE WEAVER IN THE "STAR CITY" ROANOKE, VIRGINIA

The website of Nolo Press, a legal reference for the general public, explains that juvenile cases get transferred to adult criminal court through a process called a "waiver"—when a judge dispenses with the protections that juvenile court provides. Usually, juvenile cases that are subject to a waiver involve more serious crimes or minors with a criminal history. Although being tried in adult court gives a juvenile more constitutional protections, it has distinct drawbacks too.

Some advantages for a juvenile to be tried in adult court include the right to a trial by jury with the possibility of average citizens pulled from the general public being sympathetic to a minor. In some jurisdictions where dockets and jails are crowded, the court may be inclined to dispose of a juvenile's case more quickly and impose a lighter sentence.

Disadvantages of transferring a juvenile to adult criminal court include the risk of being subject to a more severe sentence. Judges in adult court do not have the wide range of punishment and treatment options that are available to juvenile court judges—such as imposing a curfew under house arrest, counseling or community service, or confinement in a juvenile detention center instead of jail. A conviction in adult criminal court carries more social stigma than a juvenile court judgment does. Finally, adult criminal records are harder than juvenile court records to seal or expunge which makes them more freely available to the public.

Cuddy got his wish for being tough on crime in this case. On June 3, 1949, Judge J.A. Pate of the Juvenile Court conducted a forty-five-minute hearing with Captain Webb and city coroner Dr. Irvin as the only witnesses. The hearing was closed to the press. Lee Scott's mother brought her son a set of freshly pressed clean clothes to wear. She wanted "Buddy" to look his Sunday best as he was transported by guards from the city jail to the juvenile courthouse. The hearing took less than an hour to reach a decision. Judge Pate ordered the case transferred up to the grand jury. The waiver decision came just in time on Friday afternoon for the Commonwealth Attorney to submit his case to the Hustings Court grand jury on Monday morning.

The grand jury convened as scheduled on June 6, 1949 behind closed doors. They returned a number of indictments that day, not only for the Scott case. A panel of five men, with a Norfolk & Western railroad employee Walter F. Crueger as the foreman, reviewed the evidence and heard testimony from the lead detective and the city coroner. Defense attorney Messick was in court but filed no motions. The wheels of the justice system rolled forward at a rapid pace. By deciding on a "true bill," the grand jury determined there was reasonable cause for an indictment. Sixteen-year-old Lee Scott would stand trial for murder as an adult.

The trial was scheduled to begin in the Hustings Court in just three weeks. If Messick filed any motions to the court to delay the process, there is no mention of it in the newspaper accounts. He could have asked for a change of venue, that is, to move the location of trial elsewhere in the hope of finding a pool of jurors with more detachment and objectivity. Holding a trial in the town where it happened, drawing jurors from among the neighbors and acquaintances of the accused killer or the victim, ran the risk of building a jury with heightened emotions. On the other hand, perhaps Messick hoped that his flamboyant, performative style and his track record of bringing tears to jurors' eyes would win out in the end.

TO BETTER UNDERSTAND Lee Scott's journey from juvenile detention to standing trial as an adult and ending up in the state penitentiary, here is a brief overview of Virginia's court system. Each state has its own internal system of courts organized according to state laws. These systems generally resemble the model of federal courts with layered tiers of trial courts, appeal courts, and supreme courts with the final word. States can have more or less intermediate layers of courts for review or appeal. Trial courts, at the lowest level, are known by different names such as city courts, municipal courts, or circuit courts.

Virginia's court system is one of the oldest in the United States with deep roots in the English legal structure going back to the Charter of 1606 that King James of England signed to establish the first colony in North America. Almost two centuries later, at the close of the Revolutionary War, the court system reorganized to create four superior courts including the Supreme Court of Appeals which served as a model for the United States Supreme Court. Over the years, the courts in Virginia have continued to reorganize and modify their inner workings such as the number of justices on the state's supreme court or the duration of terms in office.

FLOWERS FOR DANA: THE 1949 MURDER OF DANA MARIE WEAVER IN THE "STAR CITY" ROANOKE, VIRGINIA

A revision to the Virginia state constitution in 1971 changed the name of the highest court from the Supreme Court of Appeals to its present title of Supreme Court of Virginia. The court is currently made of seven justices elected by a majority vote of both houses of the General Assembly for a term of twelve years. Although the Supreme Court of Virginia possesses both original and appellate jurisdiction, its primary function is to review the decisions of lower courts.

In a criminal case involving a felony, the accused person (if an adult) moves through several stages. First, following an arrest, the accused is either held in jail or released on bail. A preliminary hearing is held to determine if there is "probable cause" to believe the accused has committed the crime charged. Next, the case is sent to a grand jury and if they also find probable cause, an indictment is returned. Following indictment, the accused is arraigned; that is, the charges are read aloud. The accused can enter a plea of guilty, or not guilty, or *nolo contendere* (no contest.)

A trial held in Circuit Court presents evidence and hears testimony of witnesses before a judge and a jury. Felony offenses are serious crimes that may be punished either by death penalty or incarceration in the state penitentiary depending on the laws and guidelines of each state. Misdemeanors are less serious offenses carrying penalties of brief jail time or community service. The Circuit Court also has jurisdiction over juveniles charged with felonies whose cases have been certified or transferred by the judge of a Juvenile and Domestic Relations District Court. As discussed above, Lee Scott's case followed the process of a juvenile court hearing and a waiver that transferred him up for trial as an adult.

The Dana Marie Weaver murder trial was held in what was then called the Hustings Court. This antiquated legal term, carried over from England, traces back to an Old Norse word meaning "house assembly" and applied as early as the 12th Century to judicial assemblies where Anglo-Saxon kings held council and resolved civil disputes. Up until about fifty years ago, most of the lower-level circuit courts in Virginia's counties and independent cities were known as Hustings Courts. This term was gradually phased out so that by the early 1970s, only five Hustings Courts remained. Today, the Hustings Court is known as the Roanoke City Circuit Court.

At the end of a trial, a jury decides if the accused defendant is "guilty" or "not guilty" of the crime. The prosecutor who represents the state must bring evidence and witnesses to prove the accusation against the defendant beyond a reasonable doubt. A jury verdict of "not guilty" is called an acquittal and means that the criminal defendant is free and clear. The double jeopardy rule provided by Fifth Amendment to the U.S. Constitution says that a person cannot be prosecuted more than once for the same crime after an acquittal or a conviction, and it also prevents imposing multiple punishments for the same crime.

A jury verdict of "guilty" and the imposing of a penal sentence may be appealed to a higher court. In Virginia, appellate review before the Supreme Court is a two-step process in most cases. First, a petition for appeal filed with the court is assigned to a staff attorney or law clerk for research and further preparation. Oral arguments from the defendant's representative may be heard before a panel of justices, or, in some cases, by the chief staff attorney who then presents the case to a panel. The justices conduct a thorough review on the merits of each case with the assistance of detailed memoranda summarizing the facts and issues of each appeal. If the petition is denied, the appellant may petition for a rehearing. If the petition for rehearing is also denied, the appeal process ends and the judgment of the lower court stands.

JUDGE DIRK A. KUYK of the Roanoke Hustings Court was assigned to hear the case. This judge issued an announcement, in the week before the trial began, that his courtroom would be closed to the public. "All persons whose presence at the trial is not necessary will be excluded," the judge declared. No curious spectators would be allowed to watch the performance of Roanoke's most colorful defense attorney. Only the press would be permitted beyond the closed doors. City Sergeant Edgar L. Winstead was in charge of enforcing this rule.

A panel of sixty-six men were summoned to appear for the first day of the trial on Monday, June 27, 1949 to be considered for jury duty. In the process known as *voir dire*, the prosecutors and the defense attorneys held interviews of each prospective juror on the witness stand under oath. Out of that large group, only twelve men would be selected to decide the fate of a boy's life.

Chapter 10. Prosecuting the Crime in Court

IN OUR MODERN TIMES, we have come to expect the easy access to almost overwhelming amounts of information. The bulk of research involved in this project could not have been done without the internet, whereas in the past, one had to physically visit a library to dive into printed encyclopedias or crank through rolls of microfilm. Rare documents stored in dusty basement archives could only be discovered by an intrepid explorer like Indiana Jones following clues to a long-lost treasure. Yet there are limitations to what can be discovered in digitized archives. Archives of the local town newspaper, *The Roanoke Times*, are available online from 1990 to the present day. Earlier editions are only preserved on reels of microfilm stored on-site at regional Roanoke Valley libraries.

The original records of Lee Scott's criminal trial are particularly elusive. To begin with, in those days as it is today, most trial courts do not produce court room transcripts unless one of the parties specifically asks for a court reporter to do so. The requestor (usually the defense attorney) is responsible for paying the court reporter's fees. Those records, if produced, are generally kept by the attorney unless they are submitted as part of an appeal.

Fortunately, Lee Scott's father had the foresight to arrange for a court reporter to transcribe what happened in the courtroom during trial. Also, the defense attorney T. Warren Messick did indeed file an appeal after the conviction and the transcript was included with that package. The question is, what happened to the appeal paperwork?

The chain of custody ends with a clue buried deep among the governor's executive papers. In an exchange of letters dated May 1957, the Secretary of the Commonwealth had requested the entire appellate file for the governor's review. The court clerk of the Supreme Court of Appeals of Virginia sent the file with this short cover letter: "In accordance with your request, please find enclosed the petition for writ of error and a copy of the manuscript record and transcript of evidence in the case of *Lee Goode Scott v. Commonwealth of Virginia*. The petition for writ of error was refused by the Court on the 11th day of January 1950."

From this, we know that a transcript of the original trial was produced and kept with Messick's appeal. After conducting their review, the governor's office returned all of the paperwork to the clerk of the court; there is a transmittal cover letter clearly documenting the transfer. From there, the trail goes cold. Decades later, the court boxed up a number of its files for archival storage at the Library of Virginia where a majority of the cases were digitized into an online catalog. The case of *Lee Goode Scott v. Commonwealth of Virginia* is nowhere to be found among the appeals from that time period. During the research phase of this project, Kevin Shupe the Senior Reference Archivist at Library of Virginia made every effort to assist with locating this file. Mr. Shupe made a diligent search of unindexed storage boxes and reported to me by email, "I checked both boxes of original jurisdiction files that I brought over from offsite storage and did not find the Scott case file. It looks like those files have both accepted and refused cases and include transcripts. The two boxes contained cases from 1945 to 1954. They were also numbered suggesting that there was some kind of index to them, but we do not have the index."

In the absence of original trial transcripts, this book relies entirely on the contemporary newspaper accounts from *The Roanoke Times* and other publications. Journalists eagerly brought their pencils and notepads into the courtroom every day. They frantically jotted down (in shorthand) every spoken word and made note of every gesture or emotional nuance of the drama being played out before their eyes. The advantage is that their accounts will have additional information that a court reporter will not capture in typing only the dry facts of witness testimony. Of course, the drawback is that journalists are free to omit or embellish as they please for the entertainment value. After all, their job was not to make an accurate transcript but to sell newspapers.

BEFORE DISCUSSING WHAT happened at the trial, let us first have a look at the cast of characters. A number of persons inhabited the sweltering courtroom on those hot summer days. They served in the essential roles of judge, prosecutor, defense, and jury.

Judge Dirk A. Kuyk (last name pronounced "Kirk") dedicated his career to the practice of law. On the day he took his seat at the judge's bench to oversee the trial of a sixteen year old boy, he was a man of about fifty years old married to a woman who came from a prominent local family. His wife's childhood home was later sold to the city and converted into the Roanoke Public Library building. Outside of the courtroom, Judge Kuyk did not draw much publicity or attention. In his judicial decisions, however, he made a splash in 1948 when he ruled in favor of African-Americans being eligible to serve on local juries—a position he had advocated for years.

The prosecutor's team consisted of three men: Commonwealth Attorney C.E. Cuddy, a man named Beverly Fitzpatrick as Assistant Commonwealth Attorney, and a special assistant co-counsel William L. Joyce from Stuart, Virginia employed by friends and relatives of the Weaver family.

When he stepped into the courtroom, Beverly Thomas Fitzpatrick Sr. was an enthusiastic attorney about thirty years old. (As a side note, the given name Beverly was a common masculine name in the past but became more popular as a feminine name around the middle of the 20th century.) An alumnus of Jefferson High School himself, and a veteran of the U.S. Navy from World War II, he was in the early years of what would become an outstanding career in the judicial system. He served as Assistant Commonwealth Attorney for the City of Roanoke for five years and would go on to become the chief judge of the Roanoke Municipal Court—later the 23rd General District Court—in a position he would hold for over twenty-five years. After his retirement in the early 1980s, he would continue to actively contribute his time and energy to a number of non-profit civic projects and charitable causes. The father of three sons, he would live to the age of 80 until passing away of lung cancer.

Defense attorney T. Warren Messick, profiled in Chapter 9, was joined by co-counsel Keith K. Hunt. Apparently, Mr. Hunt had recently returned to Roanoke that year and was in the process of establishing his law practice in the area. One newspaper revealed Hunt as a former attorney in the Office of Price Administration (OPA) in Washington D.C. The short-lived OPA, established by an executive order during President Roosevelt's administration, had the power to place ceilings on all prices except agricultural commodities and to ration scarce supplies of other consumer items. The OPA shut down soon after World War II ended, during President Truman's administration. Hunt's other claim to fame was as a former law partner of Maurice D. Rosenberg who was a distinguished attorney and former Democratic member of the Virginia House of Delegates.

Witnesses for the prosecution were expected to be about thirty persons who held the most damning factual evidence. These included police officers who catalogued the crime scene and extracted a confession, the city's coroner who examined the body's wounds, the experts from the FBI forensics lab, the psychiatrists, and others. Frankly, the defense had very few options as the physical evidence or the basic facts of the offense were not in dispute. A confession was on file. Basically, the purpose of the trial was to determine the sentence—literally a matter of life or death. Lee Scott's father wanted as many character witnesses as possible and summoned close to a hundred people to the corridors of the courthouse. The judge trimmed it down to a list of thirty names including classmates with favorable opinions of the defendant and the high school sports coach.

Jurors came from a pool of sixty-six men called up from the community. Of those, a jury of twelve men would be selected. Note: only men were considered. In those days, women in Virginia were not allowed to sit on a jury. In fact, the right of women to serve on juries is a comparatively recent development. The 1957 film starring Henry Fonda, centered on the deliberations of a criminal jury, was titled *12 Angry Men* for a reason. There was a widespread belief in general society that women had more important duties to care for in the home or that women were too emotionally sensitive to be competent jurors. Laws changed slowly on a state by state basis, with Virginia in 1950 (the following year) allowing women to be jurors for the first time. The other states followed inch by inch until *The New York Times* ran a small column on June 15, 1968 saying, "A law making women eligible to serve on state court juries was signed today by Gov. John Bell Williams. Mississippi was the last state in the nation to take the step."

FLOWERS FOR DANA: THE 1949 MURDER OF DANA MARIE WEAVER IN THE "STAR CITY" ROANOKE, VIRGINIA

JUDGE DIRK A. KUYK banged his gavel on Monday morning, June 27, 1949, commanding order in the court. The process of jury selection (*voir dire*) occupied the first two days. One after another, the prospective jurors were interviewed by the prosecution team and the defense attorneys. Most of the men said they were parents. Several of them had daughters or sons about the same age as the victim and the accused. One after another, the men were excused if either the prosecutor or the defense found a reason to object. Several of the men were disqualified by saying they opposed the death penalty. Others were dismissed after private consultations in the judge's chambers, where Messick voiced objections that were not disclosed to the eager journalists crowding in the courtroom with their pencils and notepads.

Messick declared to the reporters that his client would plead "not guilty" and said that all Lee Scott wanted was a "fair, impartial and intelligent jury" to hear the evidence. According to the indictment, a conviction was possible under any of four degrees of homicide: first-degree murder that carried the death penalty, followed by second-degree murder, voluntary and involuntary manslaughter that carried lesser penalties.

Messick also revealed to the press that he and his family had been threatened numerous times because he undertook Lee Scott's defense. He did not elaborate on the threats beyond saying that the job of defending the boy was "not popular" in Roanoke. The attorney insisted that prospective jurors be informed of the U.S. Constitution and the laws of Virginia—that a defendant is entitled to counsel and the court must appoint someone in the event that someone could not afford a lawyer. Each prospective juror was asked directly if he bore any "ill will" toward the defense counsel.

On that first day, inside a small courtroom that would seat a maximum of a hundred persons, in the sweltering heat of summer, reporters remarked upon the defendant sitting calmly and almost expressionless. In our modern times, in the days of courtroom proceedings being broadcast on television, we have become accustomed to the subdued expression, the so-called poker face of defendants accused of horrific crimes. What the journalists felt surprised to observe has sadly become a commonplace scene in the decades since this trial.

Lee Scott wore a short-sleeved tan sport shirt, light trousers, and what are described as moccasin-type shoes. While sitting in the courtroom facing the prospective jurors and hearing their answers to his lawyers' questions, he fingered a small medallion which his mother explained was sent to him by an unnamed friend.

Mr. and Mrs. Scott sat directly behind their son to show unwavering support. They had already sent his younger sister out of town to stay with an aunt for the summer. Not only did they wish to shield the nine-year-old girl from the publicity of her brother's trial, the Scotts had been receiving anonymous death threats.

The victim's older brother Richard Weaver was the only member of Dana Marie Weaver's immediate family with the stomach to endure the courtroom drama.

Jury selection carried into a second day with more questions and more dismissals. Finally, late in the afternoon on Tuesday June 28, a jury of twelve men plus two alternates were picked. Once a jury was selected, the proceedings officially began.

Lee Scott stood up to hear the arraignment. His expression remained cool as he heard the court clerk read the indictment against him. His mother, sitting behind him, covered her weeping eyes with her hands. The accused spoke aloud in court for the first time to plead "not guilty" in a clear, firm voice.

On Wednesday morning June 29, the opening remarks began. From the prosecutor's team, Mr. Fitzpatrick addressed the jury to summarize the evidence of the case. He asked the jury to "punish Lee Scott according to the law" because the crime was a "willful, deliberate and premeditated murder." Mr. Fitzpatrick described in detail how the church's janitor found the "cruelly beaten body of Dana Marie Weaver" lying on her back in a pool of blood with her "skirt and slip up above her waist." Throughout the trial, the prosecutors would push the narrative that Dana Marie Weaver was also raped, despite the lack of conclusive forensic evidence to suggest a sexual assault. There was a gash on the girl's head, marks on her throat, and a discolored mark under her chin. The nails on all fingers of her left hand were broken off as well as the nails on her right hand's middle and index fingers. On her left leg, about halfway between the knee and the hip, was a large blue bruise which appeared to have been made by a shoe's heel. (The actual source of this bruise was never definitely identified.) Mr. Fitzpatrick said the evidence would show that Lee Scott first denied he was at the scene but later admitted to everything.

FLOWERS FOR DANA: THE 1949 MURDER OF DANA MARIE WEAVER IN THE "STAR CITY" ROANOKE, VIRGINIA

In contrast to the prosecutor's calm, matter-of-fact tone, Messick's opening remarks were full of dramatic flair. At times he almost shouted. His voice rose to its characteristic high squeak as he declared, "the evidence will show there is no question of sex involved in this case." Messick surprised everyone by conceding that Lee Scott did indeed kill Dana Marie Weaver but insisted that her death was unintentional brought about after an argument. He revealed for the first time some of the contents of that drug-induced confession, that the boy had lost his head in a brief fit of rage when the girl made disparaging statements about another youth whom Scott admired and worshipped as a hero. Messick practically begged the jury to make a finding to a lesser charge than first-degree murder. "He deserves punishment, but the punishment he is to receive is the punishment the court will tell you in the instructions you will be authorized to impose."

Newspaper reports did not mention, or perhaps they were not aware, if counsel for the defense had attempted to negotiate a plea bargain with the prosecutor. A so-called "plea deal" based on his confession would have avoided a public trial. When a defendant admits to the crime in open court before the judge, they agree to skip a trial by jury and move straight into sentencing phase. Usually, the judge presiding over the court imposes a sentence. The advantage of a plea bargain, for a defendant, is the possibility of having a lesser sentence handed down from an impartial judge compared to a harsher sentence that a jury of one's fellow citizens may impose.

Plea bargaining has existed for centuries, although in the United States it gained wider acceptance in the early 20th century as courts and prosecutors sought to address an overwhelming influx of cases. The vast majority of criminal cases in the United States are settled by plea bargain rather than by a jury trial. Plea bargains are subject to the approval of the court, however, and the rules vary between the jurisdictions in different states. For the scope of this book, more extensive research was not conducted into Virginia's plea bargaining practices in 1949; it is enough to know that he did not "plead out" to a lesser charge of second-degree murder or manslaughter after his confession. Instead, he stood trial before a jury.

Witnesses spoke in court for the first time on Thursday June 30, starting with the coroner Dr. Charles Irvin who discussed the results of his autopsy. The prosecutors continued to imply that the girl had been raped although both Dr.

Irvin and a state toxicologist Sidney Kaye asserted there was no evidence of it. Messick fought bitterly to try and prevent the crime scene photographs from being introduced as evidence but Judge Kuyk overruled.

In cross-examination, Messick asked Dr. Irvin if he saw any evidence of "an abnormal sex act in your examination of him... or the girl," to which the coroner answered no. The prosecutor asked in rebuttal, "An attempt to have ravished her would not necessarily have left signs," to which the coroner also had to agree.

Dr. Irvin declared on the witness stand that he did not believe in the youth's claims of partial amnesia. "It is my opinion that a person who remembers part of a sequence of an event could also remember all of it." To the modern eye, it appears peculiar that Messick did not take the opportunity to challenge the coroner's assertions. After all, he was not a psychiatrist or uniquely knowledgeable in that field of science. One could argue that Dr. Irvin's opinion on the veracity of Lee Scott's temporary amnesia was simply that—an opinion—and not the informed assessment of an expert.

The janitor of the church, Alexander Roland, testified about finding the girl's body in the kitchen of the Parish House on the following morning. The two Virginia Tech students testified about spending the afternoon with Dana Marie Weaver up until the time when they left her at the side door of the church building.

Many other witnesses came and went. The newspapers showed no interest in documenting each person in great detail. Friends of the defendant and friends of the victim each had their chance to speak on behalf of the either person's virtues. Character witnesses for the defense spoke of the accused's sterling reputation as a choir boy at Christ Episcopal Church, as a swim coach at the YMCA, as a counselor at the summer camp, and his other many extra-curricular activities. A next door neighbor Miss Gail Clark testified that she observed him many times playing kindly with animal pets and coaching a den of Cub Scouts in the back yard. Durwood Owens, an employee of the YMCA, said that he never heard of Lee Scott losing his temper or striking a youngster who failed to comply with orders at the swimming pool. One notable witness was Norma Balochie, a sixteen-year-old girl from Jefferson High School's junior class, who once dated Lee Scott. She testified to his high grade point average and haughtily declared, "Buddy didn't have to cheat in school. He always could learn on his own." Gossip was repeated. Tears were shed. But the star witness was yet to have his voice heard.

On Friday July 1, Messick tossed the dice in a risky gamble by having the defendant himself take the witness stand. Perhaps he hoped the jury of twelve men might feel sympathy if they could hear "Buddy's" story told in his own words. Many of the jurors were fathers of teenaged boys themselves. What parent has not experienced their child doing something wrong, who repented and begged forgiveness? On the other hand, if the defendant did not demonstrate remorse for his actions, and if the prosecutor's cross-examination showed him in a poor light, then testifying could only make things worse. The threat of a death penalty verdict remained a strong possibility.

"Something just swept over me and I hit her," Lee Scott said in court. The newspapers describe his voice as clearly audible but quavering with emotion.

"What did you hit her with, son?" Messick asked gently.

"With a Dr. Pepper bottle I had in my hand. She swung at me. I don't know whether it was her fist or a Dr. Pepper bottle. I tried to hold her and she was kicking and fell and I let go... I sort of let go and she struck some more and I held her and when she let go, she didn't move."

Messick asked, "Buddy, you didn't try to choke her to death?"

"No sir, I wouldn't choke her to death. I wouldn't have hurt her for the world."

"Did you have any intent to kill her?"

"No sir."

Lee Scott then testified he was unaware that Dana Marie Weaver was dead until he heard the news the next day. He claimed to have been "in a fog" and felt scared after their fight ended. He insisted that he was not trying to choke her to death. "I just tried to hold her."

Messick asked him to explain why he stashed a blood-stained rag in the bushes behind the home of his friend Fred Bradley. The so-called rag was a coffee urn bag that the coroner had determined might have been used to smother or strangle Dana Marie Weaver. The discoloration under the girl's chin appeared to have come from the coffee-stained fabric. Lee Scott offered a vague and feeble explanation of what appeared to be a deliberate act to conceal incriminating evidence. Once again, he struggled to recollect his own actions from that amnesia haze. He spoke of approaching the Bradley house and only then realizing that he held the coffee urn bag and soda pop bottle in his hand. He changed his mind about knocking on his friend's door when he became self-aware that his clothes were stained with blood. "I know I must have looked like a wreck."

Under a withering cross-examination by Commonwealth Attorney C.E. Cuddy, Lee Scott could not explain why the autopsy concluded that strangulation pressure to the girl's neck exceeded five minutes; at any point, he could have released his grip. Cuddy dramatically asked the jury to watch the clock on the wall and waited in silence for a full five minutes to tick by. At any point, Cuddy asserted, the youth could have come to his senses and released his grip. Lee Scott also failed to explain the bruise on the girl's thigh that appeared to be from a shoe's heel kick.

Yet he stuck to his story that he did not try to rape her. Cuddy got very aggressive to the point of harassing the defendant on the witness stand, shouting into his face. "Didn't Dana give her life in trying to avoid you?"

"She fought very hard, sir," Lee Scott answered.

"Fighting your advancements?"

"Not my advancements." He insisted that her clothing became disarrayed during the struggle and not because of him trying to rape her.

Mr. Cuddy waved an 8x10 photograph of Dana Marie's body lying on the kitchen floor, for the jury and the spectators to get a good view. Then he advanced to the witness box to confront him to his face. "Take that picture, Lee, and explain the position of her clothes." The youth lowered his head but did not pick up the photograph. Mr. Cuddy left it on the wooden railing in front of him.

His bespectacled mother arose when Lee Scott finished his testimony. She put her frail arms around her boy and helped him step down off the witness stand.

The trial's last day, on Saturday July 2, showcased the prosecutor's and the defense's final closing arguments. Mr. Fitzpatrick asked the jury to render a verdict of murder in the first-degree with the ultimate punishment. He made the argument that Lee killed Dana Marie after hitting her with the bottle in a moment of rage because he feared she would ruin his perfect reputation. He also repeated the theory that Lee Scott had attempted to rape Dana Marie and she rebuked him, that she died fighting for her honor. "This is your opportunity to take this killer out of circulation permanently. Let it be said that you did your duty here today—that you send Lee Scott to the electric chair for the murder of Dana Marie Weaver."

C.E. Cuddy added to the chorus of prosecutors' closing statements, telling the jury of twelve men that, "every so often is born an individual with a desire deep down in his heart to do things which men cannot explain... Lee fits this description."

Messick's closing statement argued that Lee Scott told a true story when he testified about striking Dana Marie Weaver after she slurred the name of a high school friend. He admired and worshipped the state champion wrestler Jimmy Webb because of his athletic prowess. Messick insisted that the boy was not trying to kill her when they fought and he pinned her to the floor. He characterized it as a "fight between two children" and asked the jury to "think back to the time when you were sixteen."

Messick pulled a metal case from the pocket of his sport jacket, unfolding it to show the jury photographs of his own teenaged children. His voice filled with passion, exaggerating his Virginia-gentleman drawl. "You are not trying a *gang-stah*. You are not trying a *mob-stah*. You are trying a youth—a boy—who, until the eighth day of May lived as close to the foot of the Cross as any human being... He is to be punished and should be punished..." In conclusion, Messick pleaded with the jury with a Biblical reference, to temper justice with mercy.

Judge Kuyk gave instructions to the jury. He gave them a limited choice between first and second degree murder. At the judge's discretion, he withheld from the jury any option of choosing voluntary or involuntary manslaughter.

The jury deliberated behind closed doors for exactly two hours and thirteen minutes. When the jury's foreman knocked on the door to indicate that a decision had been reached, the youth's mother Mrs. Scott hurried out of the courtroom. Because of her high blood pressure and frail health, she had been advised not to be present for the announcement of her son's verdict. She waited in a nearby court clerk's office until her husband came to her with the news.

The jury found Lee Scott guilty of first-degree murder. But in a small victory for the defense team, the punishment was decided to be ninety-nine years in prison. At minimum, the youth would not go to the electric chair or spend life in prison without possibility of parole. The sixteen-year-old remained stoic and expressionless as the court clerk read the verdict aloud.

As soon as court adjourned and the youth was led away, Messick immediately began planning his appeals to Judge Kuyk. He told the crowd of journalists clamoring for comments that, if he failed with the local judge, he vowed to take the case up to the Virginia Supreme Court of Appeals.

If all the appeals failed, if the conviction and the sentencing remained intact, Lee Scott would be eligible for parole after serving one-fourth of the term or twelve years, whichever was less. That is, with good behavior in the penitentiary, he could be considered for parole in 1961, what seemed at the time to be a far-off future year.

Uniformed officers escorted Lee Scott out of the courtroom and transported him back to the Roanoke City Jail, his home-away-from-home for the last few months. Newspapers reported him making an oddly flippant remark about the prospect of facing ninety-nine years behind bars. "Well, what do you think of that? How many books do you think I can read in that time?" One has to wonder if the newspapers invented this quip purely for the entertainment value.

On Sunday, July 3, 1949, Lee Scott attended church services at the city jail—now, as a convicted murderer. The next day was the July Fourth holiday, Independence Day, ironically a day when his own independence was forfeit. The last reported comment the youth made was to a police sergeant, "I've got ninety-eight more Fourths to spend in jail."

Chapter 11. Going to Jail

THE VIRGINIA STATE Penitentiary in Richmond, Virginia has a long history as an institution. Originally built in the first decade of the 1800s, the inmates were used as convict labor to manufacture nails and other products. By 1815, the penitentiary as a factory competed with other similar manufacturing businesses including former president Thomas Jefferson's nail factory that was staffed by a mixture of enslaved and free laborers. A hundred years later, in the late 1920s, the original building was demolished and a new prison was erected on the same site. The penitentiary occupied a large campus of high-walled cell blocks and administrative buildings. It was located just north of the James River on a city block bordered by Byrd, Spring, Belvedere and South Second Streets. The prison closed in 1991 and was demolished that same year. Today, the site is owned by a chemical company.

In its heyday, Virginia State Penitentiary housed—and executed—some of the country's most nefarious criminals. Former vice-president Aaron Burr was held there in 1807 for about thirty days while awaiting trial for treason, for killing Alexander Hamilton in the infamous duel. A more recent example, during Lee Scott's stay, was Henry Lee Lucas who served five years at the Virginia State Penitentiary for grand larceny. Released in 1959, Lucas later confessed to over three hundred murders committed nationwide with his Florida accomplice Ottis Toole.

Lee Scott was no serial killer but for a brief time that summer he had almost as much notoriety. A widely circulated photograph on the Associated Press wire service hit the major newspapers on July 13, 1949 as the former Eagle Scout left Roanoke City Jail for the last time to enter the Virginia State Penitentiary. One lucky cameraman snapped the shot of the convicted killer with his wrists in shackles arriving at the prison to begin his ninety-nine-year sentence. The youth carried in his hands just three things: a New Testament, a hairbrush, and a one pound box of Hershey's chocolate bars. Again, he shows his deep concern for outward appearances as he gives the cameras nothing but a cleanly dressed youth with a neatly combed crewcut.

He underwent the usual orientation for new prisoners that included an intake interview and psychiatric assessments. The initial observations recorded in his file were that Lee Scott showed "some lack of emotional concern over the offense and his predicament in the Penitentiary. He is described as having something of a 'perfectionistic attitude towards life', a 'righteous complex' and a 'limited grasp of reality.'"

About one month after his orientation, he was ready to be assigned to his first work detail. Frank Smyth, the prison superintendent, spoke to the newspapers about putting Scott to work as a clerk in the industrial division. He would be taught clerical skills such as typing, shorthand, and filing. Smyth said that his attitude was good and that he was "accepting his punishment very well." Prison officials did not expect any trouble from the youth who had no gang affiliations and no prior criminal record.

About fifty letters from all over the state poured into the prison's mail room, according to Superintendent Smyth. Some persons wanted to send Bibles, some wanted to visit the youth, and others merely wanted permission to be pen pals. All of these requests were denied, as the prison did not allow correspondence between prisoners and outsiders except for immediate relatives or friends on a pre-approved list. All incoming and outgoing mail passed under the scrutiny of censors.

Meanwhile, back in Roanoke, the legal defense team worked on preparing their appeal. The flurry of motions that Messick filed immediately after trial were dismissed by the judge. On August 30, 1949 the *Evening Star* newspaper in Washington D.C. picked up the story that Messick's co-counsel Keith K. Hunt requested a certified copy of the trial record from Hustings Court Judge Dirk A. Kuyk. This was the first step in preparing what is called a "brief" or a formal legal argument from an attorney submitted to a court.

Messick's law office spent about two months in writing their brief. A petition to the Virginia Supreme Court of Appeals was presented to Justice Herbert B. Gregory on Monday, November 7, 1949. Warren Messick himself made a presentation in person to Justice Gregory, choosing the face-to-face rather than filing paperwork with the court in Richmond. However, it was understood that the full court would be asked to review the appeal. According to what was revealed by an Associated Press snippet printed in the *Evening Star*, only one ground was set forth in the writ of error—that is, an argument for there being insufficient evidence to support a conviction of murder in the first degree.

Lee Scott celebrated his seventeenth birthday on September 16, 1949 while incarcerated in the penitentiary. By then, he had "mastered an electric typewriter...typing in the neighborhood of sixty-five (65) to seventy (70) words per minute" in performing his assigned work tasks at the prison's industrial office. Then followed the first Thanksgiving and Christmas season that he spent away from home. New Year's Day brought the dawn of a new decade—the Fifties—and just ten days later came a decision from the court.

On January 11, 1950, the Virginia Supreme Court of Appeals denied the appeal titled *Lee Goode Scott v. Commonwealth of Virginia*. An index to the Appeals of Virginia, Volume 190, holds a one-line annotation: "Writ of error and supersedeas refused." In other words, the teenager's conviction for first-degree murder was upheld.

Lee Scott settled into prison life and quietly served his time. He followed the rules. He obeyed orders. He completed the tasks and work assigned to him. A year later, he turned eighteen in September 1950 and officially became an adult behind bars. The U.S. federal census of 1950 shows "Lee G. Scott" listed on one of the ledger pages—on Line 13—among the other adult prisoners at the Virginia State Penitentiary. Such records are dry and without much detail, a list of names, their ages and places of birth. The oldest men who share the census page with him are aged sixty-one and seventy-four.

It is hard to imagine what a young man's life was like, day to day, learning to become a man in this place. A few of his thoughts are preserved in personal letters but one wonders if these documents tell the whole story. Guards watched his movements every minute of every day. Censors scrutinized every written word put into an envelope before it left the prison walls. Apparently, he chose to keep quiet, keep his head down, and not blow the whistle on the deplorable conditions in which he survived. He may have feared that his only chance for parole depended on him being a "good" prisoner.

Author Dale Brumfield discussed his 2017 book *Virginia State Penitentiary: A Notorious History* with the Virginia Commonwealth University alumni news. He explained why the American Civil Liberties Union (ACLU) called the institution "the most shameful prison in America" after a tour of the facility in 1990 just prior to the penitentiary being shut down for good. The buildings were filthy and roach infested; the summer heat was unbearable; little to no heat was provided in the winter; there was standing water everywhere; and toilets frequently stopped up. Such problems had apparently been going on for decades. Going back to the year 1968, Frank Adams, the executive secretary of the Virginia Council on Human Relations, called the penitentiary "a Dachau on Spring Street" making reference to the infamous Nazi concentration camp.

In 1971, a group of five prisoners filed a lawsuit that successfully forced sweeping changes to a racist and barbaric Virginia penal system. Author Dave Brumfeld published another article in *Richmond Magazine* that went into more detail from his interview with one of those plaintiffs. Calvin Arey was admitted to the Virginia State Penitentiary in 1965 for armed robbery. He was confined to the maximum security Building C where "poorly trained guards working with no oversight meted out indiscriminate punishments such as tear-gassing inmates inside unventilated cells, stripping them naked for days for slight infractions, removing bedding, duct-taping their wrists and ankles to the bars for days, or padlocking them inside their cells for months or even years for such bogus infractions as insubordination, sarcasm or the ever-popular 'agitation.'" The so-called hands-off doctrine held that the internal affairs of prisons were outside the courts' jurisdiction. The unwillingness of courts to defend the basic human rights of abused inmates protected Virginia's prison system—and the penitentiary's superintendent—from any outside scrutiny. Until the 1971 lawsuit shined a light on these medieval conditions, it was impossible for mistreated inmates to get a fair hearing.

From all accounts, Lee Scott was not confined in Building C with the more serious offenders or those condemned to death row. He fared about as well as anyone could do while locked inside the gray concrete walls. If he suffered any abuse from the guards, there is no official record of it. Bearing in mind that all of the records from the penitentiary were produced by, or censored by, the prison's officials, the end results show that Lee Scott was given vocational training towards a variety of occupations.

His mother passed away on December 12, 1952 and Lee Scott was comforted by an Episcopal minister Rev. C. Julian Bartlett who (many years later) wrote a letter of recommendation to the parole board on the young man's behalf. Also, he exchanged letters with his family on a regular basis, in particular his younger sister Judith who avoided publicity as she grew up, got married, and had children of her own.

Revealed for the first time, our research uncovered a treasure trove of documents from the governor's executive records. Over two hundred pages of records involving Lee Scott's incarceration and pardon have been stored at the Library of Virginia for the last sixty-five years. For the first time in print, here is a non-biased, factual account of how Lee Scott spent his time in the penitentiary.

James W. Phillips, of the Virginia Parole Board, wrote a three-page summary report on May 27, 1957 regarding Lee Scott (prisoner # 57143) to Thomas B. Stanley who was governor of Virginia at the time. Phillips reviewed the prisoner's file at the governor's request (who in turn was prompted by a letter-writing campaign by Mr. Norman Garrett Scott) but did not interview Lee personally before writing his report. He summarized the facts of the offense as recorded in the penitentiary's records including the initial intake interview. Soon after arriving at the penitentiary, Lee Scott was asked, "Now that the crime has been committed, what do you think of it?" He replied, "I don't know. I never thought of it. It just happened and I've got my time."

At the time of Mr. Phillips writing his report, about eight years into his sentence, Lee Scott had only one disciplinary mark on his record. He received a punishment in 1954 while working in the prison's dental office. "The file does not reveal the nature of it but was of approximately one month's duration and resulted in a change of assignment."

Phillips's summary also mentions the quality of Lee Scott's work ethic, which apparently was a factor weighing on the governor's mind in considering a pardon. After all, by releasing a convicted killer, one had to be sure that he would be a productive member of society. As Phillips explains, "Although at first his work was not considered to be too satisfactory, the file reveals that he very quickly became adjusted to his work and may be generally considered to have been from satisfactory to above average in his various assignments.... The most recent ratings have been excellent, with, however, the following notation: 'This man does what he is told, but nothing more even if he knows it has to be done.'"

A second report to the parole board, dated June 1965, appears to be missing the last page and is unsigned. In the opening, the writer identifies himself as the person who conducted Lee Scott's original intake. Unfortunately, there are no clues in the text as to the identity of this prison official. "On July 26, 1949, the writer interviewed the above reference inmate while he was assigned to the quarantine area of the Penitentiary. I remember only too well this sixteen (16) year old youth, who stemmed from a home of better than average conditions, was a Boy Scout with superior intelligence and a tenth grade education. I remember, too, the sternness with which he met his conviction and sentence of ninety nine (99) years and the utter lack of expression in his eyes the day of the interview."

This June 1965 report summarizes his entire time at the prison in a few concise paragraphs. This report seems to have come from an alternative reality universe that mentions none of the barbaric conditions described by other inmates. He took classes and finished high school. He learned vocational skills in the dentist's office and then in the prison's barbershop. He attended church services in the prison's chapel.

As briefly mentioned in the report below, he even took art classes and learned to paint portraits. The existence and history of art programs in America's prisons is largely undocumented. Without going too deeply into the topic, the importance of using artistic expression as a means of rehabilitation was recognized following World War II by the American Correctional and National Correctional Recreation Association. Prison art programs flourished in the Sixties and Seventies with the support of the American Correctional Association. These programs declined, however, in the Eighties and Nineties with the rising sentiment of being "tough on crime" and diminished resources. Today, most art programs in county, state, and federal correctional facilities are kept afloat through outside grants or volunteers.

One wonders if Lee Scott was given humane treatment because of his youth or lack of criminal history. Or perhaps, the watchful eye of his overbearing father made it harder for prison officials to get away with mistreating the boy. It is certainly unusual that the prison's superintendents took the youth under their wings and took a personal interest in his well-being.

As stated earlier, Lee Scott's first work assignment was a coveted, premium assignment. As a clerk in the industrial division, he learned basic office skills. The June 1965 report continues:

"He remained on this job as clerk-typist and billing and order clerk for approximately eighteen (18) months when he was transferred to the Dental Office as a clerk; however, his interest in dentistry and his ability soon found him doing the work of a dental technician, taking dental X-Rays and assisting the dentist in the performance of his duties.

"After five (5) years in this position, the subject for six (6) months was assigned to the Construction Force where he worked under the gun, outside the walls of the Penitentiary, in the construction of the new truck sally ports. He was then assigned to the Assistant Superintendent's office as a clerk and remained on this position for approximately five (5) years.

"The last four and one-half (4-1/2) years, he has been assigned to the Barber Shop as the officers' barber, a skill he learned in a relatively short period of time in the Prison Barber School which enabled him to pass the State Board examination and secure his professional registration as a barber.

"During the entire period of his incarceration, he has been punished a total of one (1) time for a relatively minor incident that occurred during his assignment in the Dental Office. Scott has developed a rather firm insight into his difficulties; he seems to have resolved a lot of the rationalization that existed at the time of his confinement. He has never been addicted to the use of alcohol and, both out and inside the Prison, has spent his leisure time in developing his mind and body, being an avid reader and one interested in sports of all types. In addition to gaining his Barber Certificate, the subject graduated from high school while in the Penitentiary, completing an extra course in Spanish, entered into and passed, with honors, the Dale Carnegie Course and the Dale Carnegie Alumni Course.

"He has been active in the Prison Chaplain's Department in working with various Sunday School groups and has been commissioned by the Department to do several paintings, a skill which he also has acquired since his imprisonment. The most recent group of such paintings was the portraits of the seven (7) Virginians who became Presidents of the United States and which were presented to the American Boy Scouts.

"The biggest accomplishment, however, has been his ability to overcome a lot of his childish thinking and a sincere effort to do the very best he could and stop trying to do better than anyone else."

LEE SCOTT'S TIME IN prison spanned the administration of three superintendents. First, the superintendent of the penitentiary since 1942, W. Frank Smyth Jr., rose to a higher position in 1960 to become director of the entire penal system. The man who replaced him as superintendent of the Virginia penitentiary was Mr. W.K. (William Kenneth) Cunningham Jr. who previously served as Smyth's assistant superintendent. The pattern repeated itself when Cunningham was promoted to director of the Virginia Department of Corrections in 1965. A man named Courtland C. Peyton succeeded him in the superintendent's chair.

Lee Scott first became eligible for parole consideration on May 12, 1961—at eleven years and ten months since he entered the prison. If granted parole, he would be allowed to sleep in his own bed, in a room without bars on the windows, with unlimited freedom to socialize with family and friends. If denied parole, his discharge date would be May 31, 2015 after serving a carefully-calculated majority of his ninety-nine-year sentence. In other words, without a favorable decision of the Parole Board, this man in his late twenties was looking at the prospect of turning eighty-two years old in a cold dark cell.

Chapter 12. Moving on with Life

IN HIS BOOK *The Body Keeps the Score,* Dr. Bessel van der Kolk, one of the world's foremost experts on trauma, speaks from over three decades of experience working with survivors. Often, people lose their sense of time passing and become trapped in a moment without any sense of past, present or future. Knowing that whatever is happening (or has recently happened) is a finite incident that will come to an end can make most experiences tolerable. The opposite is that situations become intolerable if they feel interminable—if a grief-stricken survivor perceives that it will last forever. Being traumatized means organizing one's life as if the trauma continues to be unchanged, on-going, contaminating every new encounter or event. "The survivor's energy now becomes focused on suppressing inner chaos, at the expense of spontaneous involvement in their life. These attempts to maintain control over unbearable physiological reactions can result in a whole range of physical symptoms, including fibromyalgia, chronic fatigue, and other autoimmune diseases." One reason why traumatic memories are dominant in those suffering PTSD (post-traumatic stress disorder) is the difficulty in feeling truly alive in the moment. "When you can't be fully here, you go to the places where you did feel alive—even if those places are filled with horror and misery." The doctor argues that desensitization treatment, the common psychiatric approach for PTSD, is wrong. "Desensitization may make you less reactive, but if you cannot feel satisfaction in ordinary everyday things like taking a walk, cooking a meal, or playing with your kids, life will pass you by."

Mrs. Dana Weaver

After her daughter's killer went to jail, the grief-stricken mother stayed in Roanoke and kept working in the same administrative office at Crystal Springs Elementary School. One change Mrs. Weaver made, though, was to leave the house on Day Avenue where she had spent a long, dark night pacing the floor, waiting for the girl who never came home. She moved to a new home on a different street in the Old Southwest neighborhood of Roanoke, together with her adult son who provided financial and emotional support.

Mrs. Weaver found the strength to get through the days by relying on the encouragement of her family, her friends and co-workers, and her religious faith. The first year is the most difficult after losing someone close. How much harder it is to lose a child to violence. Each milestone is a painful hurdle to overcome. Dana Marie's birthday came on July 28, 1949 when she would have turned seventeen. Her killer was locked up in the penitentiary but I imagine that gave the anguished grieving mother little solace. Instead of a party with cake and candles, Mrs. Weaver struggled to endure a painful day looking at her daughter's photographs, the blonde girl's smiles frozen in time forever young. Perhaps she made a trip to the family plot in Evergreen Cemetery to lay flowers on the bronze plaque set in the grass.

Newspaper coverage settled down and faded away as other headlines took over the nation's attention. The Cold War... The Soviets first test of an atomic bomb... The city of Berlin divided into east and west by a concrete wall... World events consumed everyone else's thoughts, but Mrs. Weaver was faced with a unique series of milestones. In September 1949, all of Dana Marie's classmates advanced into their senior year. They chose their roster of classes for their final year of high school, looked forward to graduation, and applied to colleges. The first Thanksgiving and Christmas were spent with her son Richard, himself a grown man whose courtship with a kind-hearted woman was turning into a serious relationship.

A new year came and with it dawned a new decade. As the winter's chill passed and springtime came to Roanoke, the hardest milestone must have been May 8, 1950—the one year anniversary of Dana Marie's murder. The holiday of Hallmark cards and celebration of motherhood was forever tainted by the unfathomable tragedy. Mother's Day was a time for everyone else to enjoy buying a new hat for spring weather, getting excited about new fashions in ladies' dresses, or innovations in household appliances. To Mrs. Weaver, it was the darkest date since the attack on Pearl Harbor, December 7, 1941 that inspired the United States to join the fight in World War II.

After making it through that first year, Mrs. Weaver was still on her feet, still breathing, still able to get up in the morning and carry on. Her son Richard got married but the newlyweds continued to live in his mother's house in those early years. When he saved up enough to launch into the world on his own, he found his own road to happiness with a wife and children. In the end, he managed to leave the darkness of the past behind him.

Twelve years later, when Lee Scott first became eligible for parole, Mrs. Weaver wrote a personal letter dated June 9, 1961 to James Lindsay Almond who was Governor of Virginia at the time. Apparently, she and Gov. Almond were acquaintances in the past, to the point that she refers to the governor's wife Josephine by an informal nickname "Jo." Her handwriting is a soft, gentle cursive in fading ink preserved on beige paper. Kept in a dusty box in the archives of the state Library of Virginia, these words have not been seen by anyone for more than sixty years until now.

> *Dear Jimmy, May I still call you Jimmy, as I am writing as an old friend. While I respect your high office, I still think of you as Jimmy, and could never forget the many things you have done for me, and tried to do for Murrell over the years.*

> *Wednesday night, I heard on the news report that Lee Scott has appeared before the Parole Board. The Roanoke papers have it in big headlines with much detail and you must know it is heartbreaking to have this wound opened afresh and publicized for the public.*

> *To those of us who care, we need no reminder and to others it does not matter.*

> *Surely twelve years is little punishment for the crime he committed.*

> *You said at one time, as long as you were Governor he would never be paroled. I hope you still feel the same. From many sources, from people who are in a position to know, Scott has not been a "very good prisoner" as stated in our papers. I am sure you know or can know the facts and will not consent to turning a person of his character and proven record loose on society.*

With hard work, and constant prayer for strength and faith to go on, I have been able to keep my faculties in the face of all this, plus much more than you know about.

You, I am sure do not know, that Dick lives in Ashland, has a wonderful wife and three little boys. He is now with the City of Richmond as head of the utilities department. He is a fine boy and he and his little family mean everything to me.

With best regards to you and Jo. Sincerely, Dana Weaver

Eventually, she moved to Florida and enjoyed her golden years in the warmth of tropical sunshine. She lived to the age of 83. When she passed away, her remains were shipped back to Virginia to be buried in Roanoke's Evergreen Burial Park near her beloved children.

T. WARREN MESSICK

Defense attorney Thomas Warren Messick had his own troubles and sorrows in life outside of the courtroom. Although he had spent twenty years building his career into one of the premium law firms in the Roanoke area, his personal life appeared to be teetering on the edge.

Just two weeks prior to stepping into Judge Kuyk's courtroom to defend Lee Scott, his older brother Raymond Clyde Messick had died suddenly of coronary thrombosis at the age of sixty-four. Messick took the time to make arrangements for his brother's funeral and burial, then put aside his grief while preparing to defend Roanoke's most sensational murder trial of the decade.

Following Lee Scott's conviction in July 1949, and the failure of the appeal that was denied in January 1950, Messick's home life took a sour turn over the next couple of years. He and his wife Florence separated after twenty-five years of marriage and entered into a contested battle to dissolve the union. According to an index of the public records, the final divorce decree was issued on October 3, 1956, granted to the ex-Mrs. Messick as "absolute" but without alimony.

Messick remarried in the late 1950s to a divorced woman named Jean who was a very different sort of person than the mother of his three children. As told in *Truevine* by investigative journalist and author Beth Macy, he and his second wife lived above his law office in a sprawling Victorian home near downtown Roanoke. The office was decorated with plush Oriental rugs, leather chairs, and trophies of game animals that Messick had hunted. His second wife Jean favored thick fur coats, diamond jewelry, and toy-sized dogs. Messick had a live-in maid named Pearl who was entrusted with hand delivering the annual Christmas bonuses—in cash—to the underlings in his law practice.

In early 1957, Messick accepted a case that had an equal or greater level of controversy. The year before, a jury had convicted Frank J. Snider, a twenty-nine-year old itinerant steelworker, of the abduction and rape of a nine-year-old girl. At the trial, Snider denied all the charges and maintained his claims of total innocence. He was represented by a court-appointed public defender, assisted by another attorney from Alabama. Nonetheless, he was convicted and sentenced to the death penalty. The *Washington Post* printed an interview in 1982 with Harvey S. Lutins, who became Mr. Messick's partner soon after emerging fresh out of law school at the University of Richmond. Lutins remembered Messick pulling him aside one day and saying, "'Son, we just got involved in the Snider case. Go pull the file.'"

There followed an endless stream of motions, petitions and pleadings as the lawyers worked to keep Snider alive. Local courts, the Fourth Circuit Court of Appeals, and the U.S. Supreme Court were approached for stays of execution. The lawyers argued unsuccessfully that Snider's incarceration on death row was cruel and unusual punishment and that Snider was legally insane. Arguments that Snider's trial was marred by prejudicial publicity, including a headline that referred to him as a sex fiend, also failed. Lutins unsuccessfully petitioned every Virginia governor since Thomas B. Stanley for clemency. In all, there were seven stays of execution issued by various judges. Snider's death sentence was eventually set aside, and in 1973, he was resentenced to life imprisonment.

However, Messick himself would not live long enough to see that positive development in the appeals for his most controversial client. His health failed and at the age of sixty-two, he feared that he was dying of stomach cancer. To relieve himself and his family of the expected agony of a languishing terminal illness, he made a drastic decision. One night, on February 23, 1962, he drove his car out of town. He parked on the side of a rural road near the banks of the Roanoke River, in a shady place not far from his second home. Paperwork for

Snider's next appeal, to be filed with yet another court, lay next to him on the passenger seat of his car.

Messick shot himself in the stomach and bled to death, alone.

MR. NORMAN GARRETT Scott

As the old saying goes, the Scott family's name was "mud" in Roanoke and they had no choice but to leave town. Mr. Scott gave up his home and his job as an insurance salesman. Mrs. Scott pulled her daughter Judith out of elementary school over the summer vacation. They moved away and started over in the nation's capital where they could hopefully melt into the bustling crowds on the city streets. The 1950 federal census lists Mr. and Mrs. Scott with their young daughter living in a modest brick row house in the Fort Totten neighborhood of Washington D.C. Mr. Scott found a job at a retail grocery store. Mrs. Scott, a registered nurse, worked at a hospital. They enrolled their daughter in a new school. Every so often, when allowed, they made a day trip down south to Richmond, Virginia to visit their son serving his time in the penitentiary. According to the prison's rules, members of a prisoner's immediate family could only visit for one hour every two weeks on Sundays.

In a new city, the Scotts made new friends. Much of their life is lost to the sands of time. It is luck or fate that any scraps are preserved. There is one personal letter from Marguerite Hulburt, a resident of Washington D.C., who knew the Scott family through their church affiliations. Addressed to the parole board on June 1, 1961, Mrs. Hulburt writes sympathetically on behalf of Lee Scott and his parents. She speaks of corresponding with the inmate for years at that point, although she never met him in person. Mrs. Hulburt held the opinion that he desired self-improvement and she prayed for him to have a better future. Her two-page, typewritten letter describes her efforts to solicit prospects for the young man's employment if he were to be released from incarceration. She pleads for mercy with the parole board by sharing a sentimental memory of her friend. "Lee's mother...had a most heartbreaking talk with me at one time. During this talk of one mother to another, Mrs. Norman Scott asked me if I would try to do whatever I could for her beloved son.... Mrs. Scott told me she felt she had a very short time left as she was even then, and had been for a long time, a very ill person. She died shortly after our talk. She was a very lovely person."

On December 12, 1952, just two years after moving to Washington D.C., Mrs. Scott passed away of heart failure. The brief notice in the *Evening Star* describes Myra Miller Scott as "beloved wife of Norman Garrett Scott, mother of Judith and L.G. Scott..." Her funeral services were held at St. Paul's Episcopal Church and burial was at Rock Creek Cemetery.

THE LITTLE SISTER

Lee Scott's younger sister Judith was a child when her brother went to prison. She was on the threshold of her teenage years when her mother passed away. Father and daughter carried on with life until the day she was old enough to get married and start a family of her own. One wonders how she dealt with all of it through the years. As she matured, Judith Scott must have learned to contemplate the family's tragedy and shame with a new perspective. No longer was she a small child being spirited away to spend the summer with Aunt Pat in another town. No longer was she a bewildered girl being hushed by anxious parents who were not ready to answer difficult questions. As a young woman in her early twenties, she had the maturity to plead on her brother's behalf to the Virginia State Parole Board.

In a letter dated May 22, 1961, as a young married woman with a child of her own, Judith writes: "I do have a lot to say about him. I really feel that he was unjustly sentenced as he had such a wonderful record before his trouble. What sixteen year old boy could intentionally commit the crime he did? Here is some of his life before trouble struck." She goes on to list his many accomplishments (the same list of accolades that her father often repeated) such as YMCA swim instructor, president of his home room class, Cub Scout coach, a member of the church choir with a three-year service certificate for perfect attendance, and an Eagle Scout with 54 merit badges and the Gold Palm award. In her own words, "This record above is hard to equal by any adult or youngster.

"I can't really be sure of this rumor but I want to say it regardless – I was told that there was a cousin of the victim working on the advertising staff of the

Roanoke newspaper, who covered the front page with unfavorable publicity all in favor of the prosecution.

"There are many fine Jurists who would void such a biased verdict if they would only have some assistant to review the transcript. Others have said that several of the jurors were guilty of perjury. The family uncovered the fact that the victim's uncle had two jurors who worked under his supervision on the jury.

"Whether it is a fact or not – I do honestly believe that it should be looked into. I know that he killed the girl, but the point is: was it an accident or not? Did he have an unjust sentence from what could have been 20 years instead of 99 years? Why in the world was he ever tried in Roanoke? It should have been in another city where he wasn't known and with only the facts of his case heard.

"I don't know if anything I have written will do any good, but I love my brother and will do everything I can to help him.

"I've gone through Lee's letters to me and from some of their quotes I think you will be able to see that he is not bitter from imprisonment and that he wants to join society. He's only sorry and feels that he has paid for his crime."

Her voice ends at this point, and there follows six more pages of typewritten quotes from her brother's personal letters. These excerpts of Lee Scott's letters, as selected by his sister, are reprinted in their entirety in a separate section later in this book. This single document reveals a heartwarming relationship between the two siblings with evidence that Judith faithfully preserved a stack of letters through the years. She often mailed gifts of baked goods to the prison, sent him birthday cards and Christmas cards, and occasionally visited him face-to-face. Although she moved away to another state and kept out of the public eye, Judith was apparently never ashamed of her brother.

NORMAN GARRETT SCOTT worked tirelessly every day to devise some way of overturning the conviction. Especially after his wife died in 1952, he became nearly obsessed with winning his son's total exoneration. He fell deep into a rabbit hole of paranoia, convinced that his son had been treated unfairly at trial, that injustice was done by a "kangaroo court," that the prosecutors, the judge, and the jury all had a bias for the victim's family and against his son.

He obtained the names of the jurors and investigated their backgrounds. He felt that all of the jurors were "guilty of conspiracy and all should have been indicted for perjury."

Mr. Scott wrote a letter to the Governor of Virginia on June 5, 1957 where he outlined the details of the conspiracy that he had constructed in his mind. In his own words, here is the list:

1. An uncle of the victim, Terry Wimmer, sat in that court room every day and two of the jurors who served worked under his supervision, one by the name of W.R. Shrader.
2. Friends also uncovered the fact that the Foreman of this jury, E.P. Petticrew, gave the victim's brother a position one week prior to this trial, in preference to all other applicants.
3. A fact was uncovered that another cousin by the name of Wimmer was on the Roanoke newspaper staff and printed only news which was unfavorable.
4. A juror by the name of McClellan who was qualified to serve and openly made biased statements, then was qualified over strenuous objections by the defense. Friends uncovered another fact that this juror by the name of McClellan hung around another cousin's filling station by the name of Wimmer Brothers, near McClellan's place of employment.

Mr. Scott further described, at great length, how a juror named George Boone had gossiped to other potential jurors saying that Lee's father and uncle were expelled from Stuart High School when in fact the Scotts had never lived in Stuart, Virginia. After a private consultation in chambers, the judge overruled the defense attorney's objections and seated Mr. Boone on the jury. The only concession the judge made was to instruct the other jurors to disregard any such comments as hearsay. In his letter, Mr. Scott asked the governor, "Think of this terrible miscarriage of justice. This man George Boone was again re-qualified and retired to the hotel with the other jurors to help poison the minds of others who had not openly given biased answers."

Newspapers all over the country—especially the town's local newspaper *The Roanoke Times*—dramatized and distorted the story more for entertainment value than for reporting of facts, in Mr. Scott's view. "So many friends were surprised and shocked at the unfavorable front page publicity every day..." One can clearly see by the tone of Mr. Scott's letter that his rage, frustration, and grievance was growing stronger by the day.

Apparently, he turned into a belligerent, antagonistic client of defense attorney T. Warren Messick. After the appeal was denied in January 1950, Messick disengaged from rendering any further services. Mr. Scott had paid Messick's law firm more than $5,400 for legal fees during Lee Scott's trial, which in 1949 was a substantial amount of money. An average salary was $2,950 per year and the national average cost of a new home was $7,450. From working in a law office for many years myself, this author has encountered such clients who will launch into blistering tirades on the phone; there is a widespread attitude of, "I paid you a lot of money! Why can't you produce the results I want?"

Over the next couple of years, Messick stopped responding to Mr. Scott's phone calls and letters. The final correspondence Mr. Scott received from Mr. Messick was typewritten in all capital letters—telegram style—dated January 21, 1953. "Dear Garrett: The record in Buddy's case is on file in the Clerk's Office of the Supreme Court of Appeals at Richmond, Virginia. It is available there for your use or the use of any attorney. The record cannot be taken out of the office but can be examined at any time during business hours."

In 1955, Mr. Scott lost all patience and sought out another lawyer for help. The Law Offices of Morris, Pearce, Gardner & Pratt in Washington D.C. assigned one of their senior partners John H. Pratt to examine the situation and offer advice. Mr. Pratt sent a few letters to Mr. Messick by registered mail and (except for a line-by-line itemization of $5,420 in legal services) never got an adequate response. On August 1, 1956, Mr. Pratt sent a one-page letter to Mr. Scott as a sort of final report. "At various times during the past year I have given thought to the matter of your son, Lee, and have been unable to come up with any suggested course of action which offers promise.... To sum up, while I am convinced that there is no chance for a new trial at this late date, I also believe that the only way to determine this is to examine the record on file at Richmond, where the appeal was taken. I have read the full report of the trial in the Richmond papers, which I located in the Library of Congress, and while the trial was reported fully, it is impossible to determine from a newspaper account whether or not there are errors which could be availed of at this time. I suggest that the next time you visit Lee you try to contact a lawyer in Richmond to examine the entire record for this purpose.... The only other alternative is to await the expiration of the twelve year period, at which time Lee will become eligible for parole."

THE DECADE OF THE FIFTIES came to an end. A new president John F. Kennedy was elected in November 1960 and the American people looked forward to the future. They had no idea what the Sixties would bring. Kennedy was sworn in as the 35th president at noon on January 20, 1961 to a swelling tide of optimism about the future. In his inaugural address, he challenged all Americans to be active citizens: "Ask not what your country can do for you—ask what you can do for your country." He asked the nations of the world to join in fighting what he called the "common enemies of man: tyranny, poverty, disease, and war itself."

Meanwhile, Lee Scott marked the ten-year anniversary of entering the penitentiary. No longer a teenager, now in his mid-twenties, he had learned a variety of vocational skills that would be useful if he were released into the outside world. Encouraged by the tireless crusade of his father, he held out hope for the day when he could appear before the Virginia Parole Board. With the striking of the clock at midnight on January 1, 1961, the year of possibilities would finally come.

Chapter 13. Considering Parole

PAROLE COMES FROM A French word meaning "speech or spoken word" but also "promise." The term is associated with the release of convicted prisoners who give their word, or solemnly promise, to comply with certain conditions. Parole differs from a pardon, amnesty or commutation of sentence in that parolees are still considered to be serving their sentences and may be returned to prison if they commit any violations. Referring to an informative article by Monica Steiner in the Nolo Press publication, "parole is a privilege for prisoners who seem capable of reintegrating into society. It's not a right. Although some criminal statutes carry a right to an eventual parole hearing, typical laws don't absolutely guarantee parole itself. Authorities retain the discretion to deny parole to prisoners they deem dangerous.... Commonly, after a parole board finds that a prisoner is eligible, the inmate appears at a parole hearing. If granted parole, the parolee is released and lives free in society but under the continued supervision of the prison authority."

THOMAS BAHNSON STANLEY served as Governor of Virginia from January 11, 1954 to January 13, 1958. Born in Virginia in 1890, he had a background in the private sector organizing the Stanley Furniture Company and raising purebred Holstein cattle. He began his career in politics in the 1930s at the state level and moved up to the U.S. House of Representatives in the late 1940s. As governor, Stanley proposed a higher gasoline tax and favored federal aid for the maintenance of interstate highways. He also recommended an increase in teachers' salaries while at the same time urging repeal of the state constitutional provision requiring the state to maintain a public school system. After leaving office in 1958, he returned to his furniture manufacturing business.

Toward the end of his term as Governor of Virginia, Stanley received a personal visit from Mr. Scott pleading on behalf of his son for the governor to issue a pardon. Mr. Scott brought along his nephew (his sister Eva's son) Charles Bruce McNeace who was also Lee Scott's first cousin. McNeace appears to have typed a very sloppy-looking document that the two men presented to the governor with all the solemnity as if filing a legal brief to a court. For some background on Lee's cousin Bruce, among the governor's papers is another letter dated November 29, 1965 in which McNeace gives a concise but detailed summary of his life story. He was a World War II veteran, or as he put it so colorfully, "at the age of 17, I volunteered for Uncle Sam's Navy.... I served as a gunner on a destroyer. I saw action in the Pacific, Leyte, Okinoaw [sic], Iowa-Jima [sic]. I returned to Roanoke at the age of 20, with 5 battle stars." After the war, he studied telegraphy at a university and found employment with the Chesapeake and Ohio (C&O) Railway as a telegraph operator. With all due respect to a Navy veteran and a gainfully employed fellow, McNeace was not an attorney at the railway company and did not have any background whatsoever in legal studies.

This document, transcribed below, is printed on the letterhead stationery of the C&O Railway Company although the views expressed are those of Lee Scott's father and cousin. The railway company obviously had no involvement with this effort. At the upper left-hand corner is hand-written in blue ink: "This information concerns the case of Lee Goode Scott. To Governor Thomas B. Stanley, Richmond, Va." At the very end of the document are the signatures of Charles B. McNeace and N. Garrett Scott.

The entire document is typed in ALL CAPS which makes it very difficult to read. Edits and revisions are made very clumsily by words or phrases crossed out with a series of capital X letters. I have preserved the grammatical errors, the "all caps" style and the rows of Xs for accuracy in reproduction.

ACTIVITIES...

AT THE AGE OF 16 THIS YOUNGSTER WAS...

1. THE BOYS CAMP COUNSELOR,

2. HE HELD AND WAS AWARDED SENIOR LIFE SAVING BADGE.

3. Y.M.C.A.B0YS SWIM COACH & LIFE GUARD.

4. HE ASSISTED SCOUTMASTER & WAS BOYS CUB SCOUT COACH.

5. HE WAS TRUMPETER IN JR.LEGION DRUM & BUGLE CORP.

6. HE WAS PRESIDENT OF HIS HOME ROOM CLASS.

7. HE SANG IN JEFFERSON HIGH QUARTET.

8. HE WAS AWARDED, THE HIGHEST HONORS, EAGLE SCOUT WITH ABOVE AVERAGE 52 MERIT BADGES

9. HE TOOK PIANO 5 1/2 YEARS AND ATTENDED REGULAR RECITALS.

10. HE WAS AN ACOLYTE IN CHRISTS EPISCOPAL CHURCH, ASSISTING THE PASTOR FROM THE AGE OF 12.

11. HE WAS XXXX AWARDED A CERTIFICATE AT THE AGE OF 16 FOR HAVING ATTENDED CHURCH FOR 3 YEARS WITHOUT BEING ABSENT, MANY SUNDAYS HAVING SERVED AT ALL 3 SERVICES, A LETTER & CERTIFICATE FROM MINISTERS TO CERTIFY THIS.

12. HE SPENT MANY DAYS EACH MONTH ON SATURDAYS COACHING THE CUB SCOUTS. GIVING HIS SERVICES & EXPERIENCE TO THOSE IN NEED. AND STILL CONTINUED AMONG THE HIGHEST SCHOOL GRADES.

NO ONE WITH SUCH AN OUTSTANDING RECORD OF LEADERSHIP COULD INTENTIONALLY COMMIT THE TRAGEDY WHICH ACCIDENTLY HAPPENED.

TRAGEDY...

TWO 16 YEAR OLDS GET INTO A XXXXX ARGUMENT ONE WORD LEADS ON TO ANOTHER AND ONE SLAP LEADS TO ANOTHER

THIS BOY GETS A HEAD HOLD ON THE VICTIM & HE ACCIDENTLY HOLDS TOO HARD & TOO LONG,HE DIDNT REALIZE HIS OWN STRENGTH AS HE WAS A WELL BUILT XXX BOY & AN OUTSTANDING ATHLETE

THIS WAS NOT A PLANNED & PREMEDIATED CASE...

THE XXXXXXXX... TRIAL...

HUNDREDS OF THE CITYS FINEST CITIZENS WERE IN THE ADJOINING ROOM TO THE COURT ROOM TO TESTIFY IN THIS BOYS BEHALF. CITIZENS WHO WERE CONSIDERED THE LEADERS & OUTSTANDING IN THE COMMUNITY INCLUDING, EDUCATORS, LEGAL QUALIFIED ATTYS., MINISTERS, BUSINESS & PROFESSIONAL MEN. BUT THE PROSECUTION MANAGED TO GET A CERTAIN HAND PICKED JURY.

ONE JUROR BY THE NAME OF GEORGE BOONE WAS BEING QUALIFED BY THE JUDGE & THE DEFENSE PRODUCED EVIDENCE THIS JUROR HAD ASSISTED THE VICTIMS FAMILY IN MORE THAN ONE WAY AFTER THE TRAGEDY. THE PRESIDING JUSTICE DID NOT EXCUSE THIS MAN BUT THE PROSPECTIVE JUROR WAS CALLED INTO PRIVATE CHAMBERS WITH THE DEFENSE COUNSEL & PROSECUTOR. SHORTLY THEREAFTER THEY RETURN & THE PRESIDING JUSTICE ATTEMPTS TO REQUALIFY THIS MAN FOR JURY. AGAIN HE REPEATS WITH THE EXCEPTION OF THE DEFENSES INFORMATION & PROOF OF THE ONE INCIDENT HAD HE FORMED OR EXPRESSED HIMSELF IN ANY OTHER WAY. AND HE REPLIED NO. SO AFTER HE WAS QUALIFIED TO SERVE THE DEFENSE PRESENTS OTHER EVIDENCE HE HAS CARRIED ON A CAMPAIGN IN FAVOR OF THE VICTIM. AGAIN AFTER THIS PERJURY CASE, THE PRESIDING JUSTICE DID NOT EXCUSE THIS MAN & WAS HOUSED WITH ALL THE OTHER JURY ALL NIGHT TO POISON THEIR MINDS. AND THEN THE NEXT DAY THE JUDGE XXXXX

EXCUSED HIM. XXXXX THE ENTIRE JURY SHOULD HAVE BEEN VOIDED, BUT THIS PRESIDING JUSTICE WANTED TO JOIN IN ON THIS KANGAROO TOO.

AND THE TRANSCRIPT WITH THE SUPREME COURT WILL PROVE IT ANOTHER JUROR BEING QUALIFIED TO SERVE BY THE NAME OF MC CELLAND [sic] WAS ASKED THE USUAL QUESTIONS, YOU HAVE READ THE NEWS & LISTENED TO THE RADIOS, HAVE YOU FORMED OR EXPRESSED YOUR OPINION AS TO THE INNOCENCE OR GUILT OF THE ACCUSED... ANSWER BY PROSPECTIVE JUROR, YES YOUR HONOR I HAVE FORMED & EXPRESSED MY OPINION, I AM GOING TO GIVE HIM THE LIMIT.

ANOTHER PROSPECTIVE JUROR BY THE NAME OF SOWDER, GAVE THE SAME ANSWER TO JURIST. CAN ANYONE IMAGINE HOW A JURIST COULD JOIN IN ON SUCH A KANGAROO & QUALIFY THESE BIASED ADMITTED JURORS & ARE ALLOWED XXXXX TO RETIRE TO THE HOTEL WITH THE OTHERS FOR THE NIGHT TO HELP POISON ALL OF THEM, WHICH WERE NOT POISONED & ADMITTED BIASED. THESE ARE FACTS THE DEFENSE HAD SPECIAL TRANSCRIPT MADE. XXXX HERES WHERE THE JUDGE JOINS THESE BIASED KANGAROO JURORS AFTER 3 OR 4 DAYS OF ALL THE EVIDENCE HAS ENDED, THE PRESIDING JUSTICE INSTRUCTS THE JURY THAT THEY HAVE ONLY ONE DEGREE TO CONSIDER & THAT WAS FIRST DEGREE. HE TAKES THE POSITION OF JURY & JUDGE... WITH THE DEFENSE MAKING ALL OBJECTIONS TO JURORS WHO WERE QUALIFIED WHO SHOULD NOT HAVE BEEN ALLOWED TO SERVE & XXXX THE SPECIAL TRANSCRIPTIONS WERE MADE AFTER THE ONES ADMITTED THEY WERE GOING TO GIVE HIM THE LIMIT & THE JURIST STILL QUALIFIED THEM. HE WAS OVER RULED BY THIS JURIST & OPENLY JOINED IN ON THE CRUELEST MISS [sic] CARRIAGE OF A KANGAROO OF A 16 YEAR OLD BOY. AFTER THE XXXX TRIAL & THE VERDICT WE UNCOVER THE FACTS. A FIRST COUSIN OF THE VICTIM WAS ON THE ADVERTISING STAFF OF THE ROANOKE TIMES, WHICH HE PLASTERED UNFAVORABLE NEWS EVERY DAY &

ONLY PRINTED THAT WHICH THEY WANTED & WHICH WAS UNFAVORABLE. NONE OF THE EVIDENCE & STATEMENTS MADE BY MINISTERS & OTHERS IN THIS DEFENDANTS FAVOR WAS EVER PRINTED... MANY CASES HAVE BEEN REVERSED FOR UNFAVORABLE PUBLICITY... TWO OTHER JURORS SERVED WHO WERE UNDER THE EMPLOYMENT SUPERVISION OF AN UNCLE OF THE VICTIM A MR. TERRY WIMMER. THIS ALONE WOULD VOID ANY VERDICT IN ANY COURT IN THE UNITED STATES....

THOUSANDS OF ROANOKES FINEST CITIZENS & THROUGHOUT THE STATE OF VA. WROTE OPEN LETTERS OF THE TERRIBLE MISSCARRIAGE OF JUSTICE THIS BIASED COURT RENDERED & EVERYONE SHOULD BE INDICTED FOR ADMITTED PERJURY. THESE FACTS ARE ON RECORD IN SUPREME COURT, RICHMOND, VA, & IF YOU WOULD HAVE THE TRANSCRIPT REVIEWED IT WOULD BE GREATLY APPRECIATED.

THIS BOY HAS HUNDREDS OF COUSINS WHO ARE YOUR CLOSEST NEIGHBORS & BUSINESS ASSOCIATES OF YOURS... THE TURNERS, WOODYS, WARRENS, WHITLOWS, RAMSEYS, CHILDRESES, PRILLIMANS, THORNTONS, MENEFEES, MCGHEES, DAVISES, DILLARDS, GOODES, SCOTTS, FRALINS, WALKERS...

THE DEMOCRATIC PARTY RECORDS & YOUR FILES WILL SHOW THE PARENTS & RELATIVES OF THIS YOUNG BOY HAVE BEEN THE CLOSEST OF FRIENDS & LOYAL SUPPORTERS & XXXXXXXX CONSTITUENTS OF YOUR HONOR FOR MANY, MANY YEARS.

IT IS MY FIRM & HONEST CONVICTION YOU WILL AGREE WITH ME THAT THIS IS A MOST IMPORTANT MATTER & THAT CONSIDERATION & ACTION IS MOST DESERVING, AFTER YOU HAVE READ THE HISTORY & PAST RECORDS OF THIS YOUNG BOY...

MR. SCOTT FOLLOWED up the visit to the governor with a personal letter, dated May 18, 1957, simply to say, "I wish to express to you my sincere thanks and appreciation for giving my nephew and myself the opportunity to discuss with you in person some of the facts concerning my son Lee. I will mail you another letter shortly which will contain some additional facts pertinent to my son's case, which are not contained in the official records and the transcript." By this, he apparently refers to the letter that he sent to Gov. Stanley on June 5, 1957, where he ranted for three whole pages. In that letter, he repeated the details of an apparent conspiracy by the judge, the prosecutor's team, the jury and the local newspaper to form a "kangaroo court." Scott insisted that his son was unjustly sentenced to extreme punishment and—by comparison with other cases that he clipped from the newspapers—Lee Scott should have been convicted of manslaughter, not murder, with a much lesser sentence.

On May 23, 1957, Gov. Stanley replied briefly to Mr. Scott's previous letter, "In accordance with our conversation I have requested a report from the State Parole Board, which investigates such matters for me, on the case of your son. After I have received and had the opportunity of studying the report, I shall be glad to communicate with you again."

By the governor's order, Mr. James W. Phillips of the Virginia Parole Board submitted his three-page report on May 27, 1957 as mentioned in Chapter 11. Lee Scott was not interviewed; Mr. Phillips prepared his report by studying the records on file. He read through letters from friends and neighbors that included an uncorroborated accusation "that one member of the jury stated that the boy should be kept apart from society for the remainder or greater part of his life." He reviewed the study completed by the Juvenile and Domestic Relations Court at the time of the offense and remarked upon the prisoner's claims of "unable to remember" or "unwilling to remember" amnesia blackout as an item of significance. Phillips concluded his report by saying, "The Board is not attempting to make an evaluation of any of this psychiatric or other material as to basic motives or as to type, nature or character of the individual today. If further information and more detailed study is indicated, the Board, of course, will be pleased to carry out such a request as may be made."

Gov. Stanley compared the Parole Board's factual report against Mr. Scott's wild tirades and came to his conclusion. The governor issued a letter dated June 13, 1957 and in three sentences refused to grant an executive pardon. "I have carefully reviewed the facts and file in this case, and all evidence submitted pertaining to this case. I cannot escape the fact that Lee Scott was ably represented by counsel; that the jury after hearing all the evidence found him guilty, and that the Supreme Court of Virginia refused the petition for writ of error. I do not believe the additional information you gave me is sufficient to justify a pardon at this time."

I can only imagine Mr. Scott's initial reaction at receiving this letter of refusal. Clearly, he did not take it as a hint to give up what was becoming an obsessive, paranoid delusion. One week later, he pounded the keys of his typewriter and shot back a letter dated June 21, 1957 to the governor's office. He complained about the judge who overruled Messick during the *voir dire* process, the jurors who "openly gave biased answers" and had "already formed an opinion before hearing the evidence." He maligned Mr. Fitzpatrick the assistant prosecutor by expressing suspicions for why his brother, State Senator Earl Fitzpatrick, was present at the trial every day. "What was his interest in this case?" He went on to make wild accusations, that Earl Fitzpatrick and Justice Herbert Gregory of the Supreme Court of Appeals lived in homes across the street from each other. He wrote, "I am sure they must have discussed this case between themselves many times. If these jurists had reviewed the records of the case and had given it an honest decision, they could not have overlooked the malice, bias, perjury, in the records of this case and the conspiracy that existed among that hand-picked jury." Yes, he literally said conspiracy.

Needless to say, this letter did not go over well. Gov. Stanley replied on July 3, 1957: "I have given the most careful consideration to this case and reviewed all the information time and again. I regret to say that I am unable to find justification for interfering with the sentence of the court. A member of your son's counsel visited me today and again I reviewed the case with him without finding any facts that had not been previously considered. I understand, however, that he plans to present an *habeas corpus* petition to one of the courts which, of course, he has every right to do. I hope it is unnecessary for me to add that a matter of this kind gives me the most serious concern and that whatever decision is reached is only after most painstaking study."

Stanley's one-and-only term as governor entered into its final days. By the end of the year, he would be handing over the keys to a new man.

FLOWERS FOR DANA: THE 1949 MURDER OF DANA MARIE WEAVER IN THE "STAR CITY" ROANOKE, VIRGINIA

Virginia is the only state in the U.S. where a governor is prohibited from serving two consecutive terms. Since the days of drafting the first state constitution, in conjunction with the Declaration of Independence, the people of Virginia have resisted giving too much power to one person at the top. The topic comes up for discussion every so often, and newspaper editorials fill up pages arguing for or against continuing this policy. Efforts to amend the state constitution have, so far, been unsuccessful. Every four years, there must be turnover in the executive leadership.

ON JANUARY 1, 1958 the next governor came into office. James Lindsay Almond was born in 1898 in Charlottesville, Virginia. He worked his way up the ranks in the criminal justice system, in the 1930s, rising to become Judge of the Hustings Court of Roanoke from 1933 to 1945. He won a special election to the U.S. House of Representatives and stayed in Congress until 1948 when he became the Attorney General of Virginia. From that office, he waged a successful campaign for governor. According to his biography on the website of the National Governor's Association, school desegregation was a major issue during Almond's gubernatorial term, and he supported the philosophy of "massive resistance" by ordering the shutdown of public schools rather than comply with the new civil rights laws that mandated racial integration. However, his resolve weakened after both the Virginia Supreme Court of Appeals and the U.S. District Court in Norfolk struck down the school closing law as unconstitutional in 1959, and he retreated to a program of limited desegregation.

About eighteen months into the new governor's term, Lee Scott's first cousin Bruce McNeace wrote a brief letter on September 5, 1959 to escalate his unsuccessful efforts to make an appointment to discuss the case. His letter enclosed additional materials that he described as "some facts that I know may interest you very much, also a newspaper clipping as an example of how justice applys [sic] to some." Not only did he fail to get an appointment with the governor, whatever materials McNeace enclosed with his letter had a negative effect.

The tone of Gov. Almond's reply, just four days later, shows that he felt deeply offended by the unfounded accusations of the Scott family's conspiracy theory. "While I was Attorney General, I carefully reviewed the record of the trial and its incidents. I have read the material which you enclosed with your letter. I am compelled to state that you are very much in error in your allegations relative to Kangaroo Jurors and error committed during the trial. In view of the heinous offense attended by harrowing details, I do not believe that I could consider executive clemency at this time. I am returning the material which accompanied your letter."

Another year-and-a-half passed, and on May 2, 1961 the clock struck the long-awaited hour. After twelve years behind bars, Lee Scott first became eligible for parole consideration. The Parole Board scheduled his interview for June 6, 1961. News reports broadcast this upcoming milestone. There followed an avalanche of letters that poured into the governor's office, expressing very strong opinions both in favor and against the idea of this nearly thirty-year old man going free. All of the letters obtained from the Library of Virginia's archives are transcribed in their entirety in a separate section after the end of this chapter. These letters have never been seen by anyone but the governor's staff or the officers of the Virginia Parole Board. Their opinions are their own, published here for the first time without commentary. Here in their raw form are the voices of people speaking their minds from over sixty years ago.

As mentioned in Chapter 12, the victim's mother wrote a personal letter to Gov. Almond and addressed him as "Jimmy" like a close friend. Just a few days later, Mrs. Weaver received a very warm, personal reply from the governor himself.

" Dear Dana: I thank you for your letter of June 9. I can readily understand your concern over the big splash in the Roanoke papers relating to parole consideration for Lee Scott. I doubt if there is any public official in Virginia more familiar with the harrowing details of his terrible crime than I am. I studied the record very carefully while I was Attorney General in anticipation of proceedings in the Supreme Court of Appeals of Virginia.

"I have refused to entertain any suggestion that I grant a conditional pardon. Under the law it is routine that the Parole Board give consideration to those whose eligibility for consideration is defined by law. I, of course, as

Governor cannot under the law direct the Parole Board with reference to matters coming under the statutory jurisdiction of the Board.

"Scott's crime was one of the most violent and reprehensible in the annals of this Commonwealth. I have heard from a great number of citizens, who constitute the finest among our people who believe in justice and right, who fear that a parole for Scott at this time would not be in the interest of law enforcement or the public good. Without any sense of prejudice on my part, I feel the same way about it, and I shall let the Parole Board, with due deference to its responsibility, that it is my earnest hope that a parole not be granted.

"It is always nice to hear from you. Jo and I hope that we will have the privilege of seeing you in the near future."

THE PAROLE BOARD DENIED Lee Scott and sent him back to the sliding-bar gates of the penitentiary. Newspapers carried the story at the end of the month, again rehashing his crime and informing the public that he would become eligible for consideration the following year. Those who wished for him to stay behind bars marked their calendars.

Mr. Scott reached out to the governor who (like his predecessor) was coming to the end of his one-and-only term in office. On January 5, 1962, Scott typed a two-page letter to Gov. Almond on the letterhead of The Massachusetts Protective Association, Non-cancellable Accident and Sickness Insurance; his name pre-printed on the stationery as Norman Garrett Scott, Special Agent. One wonders if the insurance company ever knew of their employee using business stationery for a personal matter.

"My Dear Governor: It is hard for me to realize that more than thirty years have passed since my parents purchased the Old Huff property on First Street, which was next door to another fine young man starting on his way up, one who was deserving of all the success he had bestowed upon him. Even though we only lived at the First Street a short time and sold this property to purchase the old Dr. Hurst property on Highland Street Highland Park. In the short period we lived next door to the Minters and Almonds, we felt honored to have such fine neighbors.

"Governor Almond, it also has been more than thirty years that I used this same stationery writing you a short note congratulating you upon your being selected to the Hustings Court Bench.

"Governor Almond, I am enclosing you a list of some of the fine and worthy activities in which my son Lee took such an active and regular part prior to and including his 16th year of age. It is my hope and prayer that you will give this young boy your favorable consideration and allow him to have a chance to return to fine and worthy activities he was so interested in, and too, while I am able to give him some assistance for the future and his welfare.

"I have been aware of the tremendous number of problems your office has faced since you have been in office. Was my reason why I have not attempted to include additional ones for you. I am sure no other Governor had so many while in office.

"With my kindest regards and every good wish for the New Year."

The governor replied on January 9, 1962 with a terse statement: "During the few remaining days of my administration, it would be utterly impossible for me to review this file." So ended the term of a second governor to refuse Mr. Scott's pleas for clemency.

WITH THE NEW YEAR 1962 came a new man to sit in the governor's chair. The cycle repeated itself as Mr. Scott wrote letters and appeals for executive pardon, off-set by an outpouring of letters from concerned citizens of Roanoke. Year after year, an annual event rolled around like a dismal local holiday known only to the grieving families and distraught citizens of the town. Every year in the month of June—in 1962, in 1963, and in 1964—the ever-aging Lee Scott appeared for an interview with the Parole Board. Every year, he was denied.

Across the years, more letters poured into the governor's office that expressed opinions for and against the release of the man who killed Dana Marie. These are also transcribed after the end of this chapter. Except for the dates of posting, the sentiment in those letters did not change with the passing of time. The voices are speaking through their written words of a pain that will not heal, of a grief that cannot be overcome. After more than fifteen years since the girl's body was discovered on the floor of the kitchen, the agony remained as fresh and raw as the day it happened.

If the parole board—again and again—refused Lee Scott a chance to live outside of the penitentiary's walls, then his fate rested in one man's hands. Only the Governor of Virginia has the executive power to issue pardons or stays of execution, overruling with the stroke of a pen the decisions made by judges.

Letters

Personal Letters from Lee Goode Scott to his Sister (Excerpts Selected by Judith Scott) Dated Between September 1956 and May 1961

DATE (9-18-56) BIRTHDAYS here are strange in many ways, the only difference from an ordinary day is I know that it is special along with a few others outside who share the thought. This eighth one here makes me realize that I remember almost here as at home.

(10-29-56) How many times I've wished the public could forget as easily. However, at least I can get out and walk in the yard at night, when most everyone else is cooped up. Moving around at odd hours could be a bad habit for I understand that men on parole have a schedule, in some cases as bad as a new baby's.

(12-24-56) ... Yesterday Rev. Seiler was over to wish me a Merry Xmas. We talked of many things, the most important of which was centered on you. He didn't mind my acting like the first uncle in the world but he had to laugh when I showed him pictures just 10 yrs. old, (when we were in Fla.) and explained that just a little freckled-faced girl made me feel ancient. I have received many cards so far and it makes me feel wonderful to know that I have a few friends. Everything is going my way and this is a swell manner in which to leave the old year.

(1-21-57) Rev. Seiler came over the first Wed. instead of the second, to give Communion. It was a right good way to start the new year and I was happy to talk with him later and brag about being an uncle. One sad note, Rev. Ostergrew resigned and I don't know who will be the new Chaplain.

(3-4-57) As it just so happens the middle of last month was during one of those long breaks between mail and I was brooding over the fact that since I'm not able to write but once a week, how can I expect more. When your Valentine card came in everything was changed around. Last Sunday I got out on the recreation field for the first time in a couple of months. It felt good to stretch my legs, feel the sun nice and warm and have dirt under my feet. It's right hard to explain the ache that comes from missing such ordinary things.

(7-8-57) Since your trip down here Wed. I have been waiting for the regular paper that is given out each weekend for the mail, to be able to tell you how happy I was to see you and how much I enjoyed the visit. I can't tell you how much of a thrill I got out of holding him but I was afraid he would fall if I didn't hold him firmly and on the other hand I feared hurting the little fellow. The people who met you and saw him were certainly impressed and later on couldn't help but smile when speaking of his cute appearance. Of course, there is one thing bad about such visits and that I'm sorry to see you leave but the goodness of the visit more than compensates.

(8-19-57) As easy as I get along during hot weather I suppose I would do well in Wash., anything that would be outside could beat the conditions that prevail. Having a job offer like the one you spoke of doesn't mean that is what I'll do, it all hangs on what the parole board thinks is best and they do the deciding, no matter if I make a pardon this year or a parole 3 yrs. from now when I'm eligible for such consideration. Sort of the same thing I told Aunt Pat when she wanted to help, to write the board so they will have the information on file when a decision is made.

(10-7-57) The last week in Sept. I had a surprise visit from Rev. Tatnall and his assistant Rev. Joy. One of the first things I wanted to know was if they had any difficulty gaining entrance. Both said they were lucky and remembered to carry their credentials with them. Of course, I wanted to hear about St. Paul's but it was two against one and the subject stayed on me most of the time.

(12-2-57) Of course when Thanksgiving comes around I think of the grief and trouble I've caused Dad and you and I feel sorry. That evening is my day for resolutions, not New Years Day, and I think what will be done by me and what won't and what I should like to do. Even though you tell me the past is over, I can't help brooding or ending it with plans for the future.

(2-24-58) Work has started on the Chapel. Even heard a rumor that the bars would come out of the windows, why bars were needed in the first place I'll never know.

(3-17-58) This week I almost put off writing but got to thinking about your birthday and not being able to send you a card, I decided a letter a few days early wouldn't make any difference. I do hope you all haven't given up the home building idea you so clearly confided to me when you were here last year. If building your own house is what you want to do, stick to it! It would be softer and easier maybe but many times the easy way isn't the best or for that matter the most desirable, few things can compare with doing a hard job well.

(4-26-58) Thanks for sending the Easter card. I can always count on you to remember and small things do mean a lot.

(9-27-58) Last week I had a nice birthday which was made better by receiving the card from you all and the letter with the clippings and the picture of Ray. Also received remembrances from Dad and Aunt Pat. In fact I can't think of anything that went wrong with Tues, or that I could complain about considering the circumstances.

(10-28-58) Governor Almond is everything Gov. Stanley wasn't, a good administrator, wonderful speaker, and already pardoned more men than Stanley did in 54 yrs.

(12-22-58) This time of year is certainly the best for me. Few things go wrong and to qualify that, when they do, they don't seem to make much difference anyway. While wishing, may this holiday season be a happy one for you, your husband and children. Merry Xmas.

(2-14-59) In daily life, at work, on the recreation field, in my room, while reading or listening to the radio, even watching TV in the attempt to fill every moment with something that must be done, seen, said or planned, I seem to lose because of not taking time to be quiet and just think. It is a predicament because if I stop or slow down, I become aware and when not controlled, my mind forgets the blessings I have and concentrates on what I lack, freedom. Even though I'm cut off from you, my heart isn't here, never has been, but I make the best of a bad situation and try to take advantage of any good condition.

(3-16-59) A good example is a fellow who was convicted of first degree murder, armed robbery and burglary and sentenced to 48 yrs.

(4-13-59) I no more premeditated a crime or think of myself as a murderer than the person who said, "I didn't know the gun was loaded." But who will believe this if they prefer to believe something else?

(5-31-59) As I sit here this rainy Sunday it hardly seems you and little Ray are so far away and that I won't be seeing you all tomorrow. Of course, I really don't feel that you are so far away because the mental pictures that are imprinted in my memory are of such beauty that they will never fade. I like to think that you all had a good trip back home and found the rest of the family was alright. Maybe you postponed your letter but this one has to be censored tonight and I can't and don't want to wait until next week-end to tell you how much I love you.

(6-29-59) I am really surprised you really liked the paintings I've done, perhaps because I know the mistakes. You know the one of Dad I had help on, but the others only advice and not much of that.

(8-17-59) With my parole eligibility coming closer (1961) I am happy that the recession has evened out and things are looking better. It's hard enough to keep a job held open for months during good times while the board makes up its mind and I've seen many a man denied because suitable employment wasn't available.

(10-5-59) I don't know when I've enjoyed homemade food more. You sent such a large package, I started to put half in the ice house but changed my mind and took a quarter of each and the rest is on ice. The cheesecake is swell, some people make it too tart. (I guess from fruit juice), yours is just right. There is a fellow down the hall, from Portland, Maine who has mentioned his liking for blueberry muffins, in some conversations. He's a pretty good guy so I let him live a little and gave him some.

(11-30-59) All this month I had been expecting Dad to drive down from Wash. and late in the afternoon two weeks ago when I figured the trip had been postponed again, I got a call from the switch-board to come to the front. Virginia had come along and although this was just her second time, I was glad she made it for it was a pleasure to see and talk with her. Bruce has done quite a bit for me and it was very easy to sit down and write a letter expressing my appreciation for all his time and effort. But it wasn't so easy to type the last letter I sent. Dean Bartlett's wife recently died. Perhaps you know she had suffered a heart attack a year or two ago and was ill.

(1-11-60) Of your attributes that I admire the most is your generosity and kindness. Here I was trying to figure how I could send you all something to secure that lot and at the same time you wanted to establish an account so I could obtain Clothes on my release.

(2-15-60) Of my fondest memories are those when returning home from school I would find Ma sewing. I would sit and watch or bring in my lessons and do them nearby. She had that old Singer and she could make almost anything with it. To me it was fascinating to watch and marvel how she could use both hands on the cloth and regulate the speed with the foot peddle. She would swell my ego by asking me what type materials and colors I liked.

(3-14-60) This evening it began, a couple of inches covered the walks quickly and without considering the fellows who would be doing the shoveling in the morning. I made a trip to see some fellows in the dormitory, trusty quarters. The trip took a little longer than usual because I hadn't heard snow crunch and pop so loud in a long time.

(4-11-60) Three weeks ago Rev. Seiler came over to see about baptizing a friend and brought an artist-priest friend with him to look over a couple of paintings. They are amateurish as you can guess and then too, they are out of style, no abstract ideas or weird symbols. In fact, a squirrel in a fall forest scene looks exactly like a squirrel in a fall forest scene, corny, huh? But they brought two wonderful books on painting and drawing that are just what I need. No, that isn't exactly right, what I need is talent and speed. Lacking these two items I'll just keep my painting a pleasant hobby. It should fit right in with parole conditions, stay off streets, be in at a certain time, etcetera.

(8-8-60) However, I'm a good barber and if you'll [check] the want ads you will see there are numerous openings available. This simplifies the matter of a job. The next point the board considers is who will act as sponsor and if they are out of this state, will that state accept the parolee. The board likes to have more than one plan to choose from and Aunt Pat gives them a second choice.

(9-26-60) Thank you for sending the birthday card, it made a good day better. Some that I received were early or others coming late made the day last longer and of course I was pleased with those that weren't expected. Of my twenty eight this makes twelve here, almost half my life inside these walls. It's difficult for one to say he's glad to see them go by and then have less time to do or is sorry to have the years go by with nothing definite and see so much waste.

(10-10-60) I certainly have been having some wonderful after-meal desserts these past few days. I took your advice to go easy on the brownies, not because of worry of stomach ache but rather that they are so delicious and preferring to make the flavor last. It isn't wise to publish the news of treasure but a few friends celebrated with me and I believe praises of your cooking would have swelled your ego to the point where you would have any ole toothache. One of the foreigners down here, a Maine boy, certainly was impressed with the blue berry muffins. I have enjoyed all that you baked and I can't think of one thing you could have added to make it or my birthday any better, thank you.

(12-19-60) Mr. Cunningham gave me the newspaper clipping that tells of the portrait I painted. Actually it tells very little but it's the first time in over twelve years that my name has been connected with anything good in newspapers (the 8 president's portraits writings mentioned no names) and it makes me feel fine. Since it connects with a Masonic Lodge, Dad would like to read it and you might forward it on to him.

(1-9-61) Rev. Seiler says that I'm going to have a hard time adjusting to all the change that has taken place these 11-1/2 yrs. I will enjoy having the opportunity. What I like is his speaking as if it is a fact that I will have the chance. Happy New Year.

(2-20-61) You come up with some good ideas, Judy. There's nothing I would rather do in my spare time than paint. You make it sound even better saying, After you're out. Then there will be better materials and opportunity and I can really do a family portrait.

(4-10-61) A couple of weeks ago I moved up the hall from 19 because of planned expansion of the hospital lot which is only a wall away. The move was to my advantage as this room is wider and with the favorable window location it is better for painting. Moves involve a lot of work such as the nail holes filled with plaster preparatory to painting. Repairs are easy when there is the thought that I may leave it for someone else and this is only temporary quarters. Excuse me for indulging in day dreaming.

(5-13-61) They don't usually change court location unless you can't get a fair trial and that is water under the bridge.

Letters from Concerned Citizens, Relatives of the Victim, or Friends of the Prisoner, Addressed to the Governor of Virginia or to the Members of the

Parole Board, Preserved in the Governor's Executive Papers, Dated Between May and June 1961

Roy L. Garis, Professor of Economics at the University of California, typed a two-page letter to The Parole Board, Va. State Penitentiary on May 17, 1961

Please permit me to identify myself. I was born and reared in Roanoke, Va. I have a B.A. (1919) and M.A. (1920) degree from the University of Virginia and a Ph.D. degree from Columbia University (1927). I have taught in three summer schools of the University of Virginia and in William and Mary (Norfolk) in the summer of 1959. This is my 40th year of college teaching. I have been Professor of Economics in the University of Southern California since June 1946. I am also National President of the Order of Artus, national honorary economics fraternity. I was appointed to one of the Governors Commissions by the Governor of Virginia when Virginia had its recent celebration, and I am now on the Governor's Commission to deal with problems of the aged here in California.

I set up the social security system, public assistance division, in Tennessee and administered it during its first two years, 1937-39 while teaching in Vanderbilt University in Nashville. As Assistant Commissioner of Public Welfare and institutions, I had all of the state's public penal institutions, including the penitentiary, reform schools etc. under my jurisdiction, and know these problems very well including parole. For this work I was appointed a Tennessee Colonel by the Governor of Tennessee, Gordon Browning. (See Who's Who for other details.)

I deal with the problems of young people daily. Here in California I see young people - called boys by the press - 16 to 25 years of age, who commit many serious crimes including murder, who are too often given a slap on the hand and told to be good boys in the future.

Even murder gets only one to three or four years. There is no serious punishment. I would not have such a policy in my native Virginia. But I have given much thought for years to the case of Lee Scott in your institution.

He was perhaps 15 years of age at the time. He was a churchgoing boy - in fact his crime was committed in a church house. I knew his parents well as they lived next door to my parents for several years. I have never believed he intended to kill the girl. But that is not for me to say.

He has been a model prisoner. I wish my graduate students could write in the beautiful English he has learned while confined. He is soon to be eligible for parole. Society has nothing to gain by continuing to confine him in the penitentiary. This young man will be a good citizen if returned to private life. He could join his sister in Massachusetts or his father (I believe in Washington D.C.). I would advise him never to return to Roanoke.

Compared to some here who are never punished even for murder and only lightly punished at that (Dr. Finch can get out in seven years here), he deserves favorable consideration from your parole board. Again I say, society and Virginia have nothing to gain by refusing him parole. He has paid for his impulsive act. His mother died as a result of its sorrow.

With my years of experience behind me, I urge you to parole Lee Scott (57143) when his name comes before you in the near future, for I believe his record in the Virginia Penitentiary justifies it. When a debt is paid by a prisoner who has conducted himself well, I am convinced he should be paroled.

I pray that you see it that way too. I beg of you to release Lee Scott that he may start a new and worthwhile life (outside of Virginia).

P. S. The wife of your Governor and I were reared together in Roanoke. The Governor and my family have been good friends for many years.

Mr. and Mrs. Harold Hurlburt, living in Washington DC, typed a two-page letter to Mr. Charles P. Chew, Director of the Parole Board, on June 1, 1961

After many years of corresponding with Lee Goode Scott I have formed a most favorable opinion as to his potential character. His letters have indicated a creative intelligence and, as the years have gone on, a maturing mind. I have been more than pleased, many times, to read in his letters a desire on his part for self improvement and a most gratifying - to us - happiness in his Church affairs. All of these things, and many more will, I hope and pray, add up to a possible future contentment, happiness and an earned place in a world of human affairs for a boy (young man) who has known great sorrow. That is, indeed, and shall continue to be, our earnest prayer for Lee Goode Scott.

Lee's Mother, whom I knew through our Church affiliations, had a most heartbreaking talk with me at one time. During this talk of one mother to another, Mrs. Norman Scott, asked me if I would try to do whatever I could for her beloved son. (Lee, from his record, as a lad, was quite a creditable person not alone to himself but to his parents. I feel sure you have a full record of his participation in many worthwhile endeavors for youth. It is all greatly to his credit.)

Mrs. Scott told me she felt she had a very short time left as she was even then, and had been for a long time, a very ill person. She died shortly after our talk. She was a very lovely person.

Since finding that Lee's case would come before your board sometime within the near future, I have done what I could to solicit what aid was seemingly available. I contacted a Mr. Freeland of The Salvation Army - This is Mr. Freeland's line of work with the Army -

and he told me he would come to see me and have a talk as soon as he could. Of course he could promise nothing at this time. I talked with Canon Richard Williams of The Washington Cathedral - He also works along this line of helping in rehabilitating those whose cases come to him for help. He told me he would look into this and would, of course, do what he could. I have asked some of my close friends to be on the look-out for any possible position which would be right for Lee until he gets a sort of grip on the world outside. It is bound to be a jolt to Lee for a time, at least. But I believe he is a fine young man. He will make it. I have no doubt.

My husband, Harold, was told of Lee by the Very Rev. C. Julian Bartlett, now Dean of Grace Cathedral in San Francisco, California. The Rev. Bartlett was at one time our Rector at St. Paul's Rock Creek Church. He felt great interest in Lee and visited him many times. Through him, Lee became a member of The Brotherhood of St. Andrew and Harold, along with the other members became interested in his case. We have discussed it with some of these members and they are willing to do what they can to help Lee.

If there is anything we can do of any different nature than we have done and are still trying to do, we will be happy to have any suggestions along the line which you may feel would be of possible benefit to this young man whom we call friend and in whom we feel great interest.

May God continue to guide you in this wonderful work you are doing and in your efforts to judge fairly and well all those who look to you for help.

My husband is in full accord with what I have written to you, and thanking you for your attention, I remain, Very sincerely yours,

Mr. John H. Parsons used his own company's letterhead (the John Hughes Co., with offices in Washington D.C.) and typed a letter to the Virginia State Parole Board on June 1, 1961

I am writing you in the hope that Lee Scott will receive the utmost consideration for a parole. On two occasions I visited the prison in Richmond but could not see Lee. I have never met him, but feel as though I had. This is because I have read letters he has written, talked with men who have visited him, known other members of his family, and have a knowledge of the circumstances of his imprisonment.

Altogether I think he would be a useful and successful member of society. As the owner of a small business (45 employees), if it helped any, I would be glad to interview Lee to see if he would work for us in some capacity. If there is anything I can do to help in your arriving at a decision, I would be pleased to do so.

Mr. William D. Dooley, living in Roanoke VA, typed a letter to Chairman Virginia State Parole Board on June 8, 1961

I am writing this letter as a Citizen of Roanoke and one who feels the parole of an inmate of yours, Lee Buddy Scott by name is strictly bad taste and against all the good graces of society.

I grew up with the deceased, Dana Marie Weaver. Dana and I played together as children. I knew her whole family and she was well thought of by all in the Grandin Court section during that or those early years. I am sure her brother Reginald who died in the defense of his country on Iwo Jima would turn over in his grave if he knew what happened, let alone now Lee Scott being set free.

I feel that Lee Scott was given a fair sentence and very lenient at that, for the terrible crime he committed. I am sure some feel he should be freed, but, I don't know who. He, in my opinion has lost his right ever to live in a Society such as ours again. I think to release him on Society would be as bad almost as the Crime he was convicted.

I am sure the newspaper prints many things that are or can be taken two ways. The Roanoke World-News today, stated what all Lee Scott had done while in the "Pen" but, it did not say of the trouble he had gotten into while he was there either. I heard of two incidents in which he was involved, and I was in New Orleans in the Seminary at the time. It matters not to me necessarily whether these be true or not, my opinion is still the same, he should be kept within the walls at Richmond until he is too old to do or go anywhere else.

It is fine he has a trade, he can use it on his fellow friends there, if he has any. I surely would hate to be guilty of being or serving on a Board who is in favor of releasing such a person on Society again. He didn't get what he deserved, but, he should serve what he got.

I along with others are writing to ask that you please not release such as he on Society now or at any time. We hope you will at least ask God to help you in making such a decision. I hope this letter will help someone to see our view in the outside world. Thank you kindly.

Mrs. W.G. Nelson Jr. living in Roanoke VA wrote a letter to Charles P. Chew, Director of the Parole Board, on June 8, 1961

Word that Lee Scott, who murdered Dana Marie Weaver in cold blood, may soon be paroled and allowed to roam the streets and again frighten women [*unreadable*] while wearing a mask and do other frightening things, strikes terror to my heart. I would not want to deprive anyone of freedom but for Lee to be wandering around Roanoke, or any place else, is a threat to everyone else. In addition to having strong hands which he used to strangle rabbits before he killed Dana Marie, he has now learned to barber and to use razor sharp instruments. Has he given any indication that he has been changed inwardly so that he will not use his old & new skills to hurt, maim or kill people?

I beg of you please consider well before releasing this warped personality and keep him under constant surveillance.

Sincerely & deeply concerned.

Dr. Daniel R. Miller, a dentist in Roanoke VA typed a letter to Governor J. Lindsey Almond on June 8, 1961.

This is a letter of recommendation for Lee G. Scott inmate No. 57143 who is now eligible for parole from the State Penitentiary.

I first met Lee when I was Dentist at the State Penitentiary in 1951, where he was my dental assistant and a very excellent and conscientious one.

We have corresponded, and I have visited Lee over the last ten years, so I feel that I know him better than any person; certainly anyone outside the Penitentiary.

I feel he has made an excellent adjustment in being punished for a crime, First Degree Murder? He has made a great religious contribution in the service he had rendered in the Chaplains program at the penitentiary.

I am convinced that if released on parole, he will make a citizen we may all be proud of. Over the years, his letters indicated deep perception and an esthetic quality very few possess.

I sincerely hope he may be granted this opportunity he so strongly deserves. Undoubtedly this is one inmate the state will never have to spend funds for again.

If I may be of further aid as a help in his rehabilitation or adjustment to society after his release, I will be glad to assist.

Mr. and Mrs. H.R. Pedigo, living in Roanoke VA wrote to Mr. Charles P. Chew, Director of the Parole Board, on June 12, 1961:

> We are of the sincere opinion that (Buddy) Lee Scott, who murdered Dana Marie Weaver twelve years ago, has not changed enough to be turned loose on society again. The fact that he has changed "jobs" so many times there in prison proves very definite [sic] that he is having difficulty in adjusting his life.
>
> Will you, for the sake of society as well as for Buddy Scott's sake use your influence to see that he is not given his freedom. It is up to you to see that this boy is not tempted again to commit another awful crime.

Mr. W.J. Miller, living in Christiansburg VA wrote to Mr. Charles P. Chew, Director of the Parole Board, on June 12, 1961

> It is reported that parole of Lee Goode Scott, No.57143 is under consideration.
>
> In considering the parole of such brutal slayer, I can't help but implore that the safety of innocent persons should receive paramount consideration. Lee Scott not only murdered an innocent person, but I am told that the punishment he inflicted upon the innocent girl victim was worse than death; that she was bloody from her waist to her knees. In other words, as typical of a sex-maniac, he gratified himself by inflicting the fullest extent of punishment possible. Yet he faced his classmates in school the following day with the conscience of a habitual criminal. Not only did he take the life of an innocent person, but he took from the victim's mother the zest of living, as well as no doubt shortened the lives of others. Lee Scott demonstrated by the nature of his crime that society would live in fear in his presence.
>
> If parole would serve the welfare of Scott and the public in general, I would not in any manner oppose his release. In this connection, I am

enclosing newspaper clippings which establish beyond a reasonable doubt that parole is not the solution for such criminals. A 16-year-old boy who was released from reform school just four months shot and "...killed a policeman who came to the aid of a 13-year-old girl he was attempting to assault."

In another case, a rapist who had been paroled about one year, "...Brutally beat and raped a 40-year-old white woman in a Charlottesville parking lot."

In another case, a convicted rapist confessed killing an Indiana girl, 11-years-old. "State police records show Hashfield was sent to the Indiana Reformatory on a rape charge in 1929 and again in 1936 on a charge of assault with intent to rape. He was sent to prison in 1947 on a charge of sodomy involving a juvenile and had been paroled three times since then..." (Emphasis supplied) I

In another case, A parolee-rapist attacked a Madison College teacher.

In another case, "Recently Paroled Killer Claims Two More Victims."

In another case, "An Air Force veteran first arrested for molesting a child 12 years ago admitted today the sex slaying of John Dudko, 10, and a sadistic attack on another boy."

At the time of Scott's conviction, people were afraid that he would, "..Serve a few years and be turned back to society a polished criminal." I have talked with a number of people and their sole concern is, "The safety of society and the safety of women."

Lee Scott demonstrated that he was cruel and cunning, but all that I do is to concur in the wishes of many in asking you, "Please do not expose this man to society."

Please refer to my letter of November 1, 1951 and if you do not have the letter, let me know and I shall gladly furnish you a copy thereof. Very truly yours

Dana Marie Weaver's maternal uncle Mr. Terry W. Wimmer, living in Roanoke VA wrote to Mr. Charles P. Chew, Director of the Parole Board, on June 12, 1961

No doubt this will be but one of many letters you will receive regarding the review of the Lee Scott case for parole, but since I am the uncle of the little girl he brutally killed, and sat through the agonizing trial, I feel impelled to add my protest against releasing this man. His attitude throughout the trial clearly indicated his sadistic, unrepenting and arrogant nature, which was widely discussed at the time.

It is my sincere feeling he would be a hazard to any community, and so short a term for such a heinous crime would be unthinkable and damage respect for the justice of the courts. The people of Roanoke are very much disturbed that there is any possibility of Scott being paroled. I realize that under the penal system procedure his case automatically comes up for review at this time, but certainly hope that the Board will not approve parole in view of the enormity of his crime.

Dr. Charles S. Maas, a dentist with offices in Roanoke VA typed a letter to Chairman, Virginia State Parole Board on June 12, 1961

As an interested citizen, I beseech you to not release Lee G. Scott from prison.

He was convicted of performing the most heinous crime in the history of Roanoke. He was a friend of mine, and the young lady that he murdered was friends of mine, also.

During the summer of 1957, I was employed by the State of Virginia as a dentist in the State penitentiary. During that time, I saw a good deal of Lee. He still talked of the crime as if it were some feat to be admired. He spoke of returning to Roanoke. We don't want him! The sentiment against him was violent in 1949, and I feel that it has not diminished a great deal in twelve years. A petty crook may be rehabilitated in prison, but not a psychopath.

I could go into specific details about his life in prison, but I am sure you will receive an objective, true report from Mr. Cunningham.

Mrs. Marcia L. Larson, of Fishburn Park School, Roanoke VA wrote to Mr. Charles P. Chew, Director of the Parole Board, on June 13, 1961

As a citizen of Roanoke, the Sunday School teacher of Dana Marie Weaver and a city school principal who works with the youth here and for their future, I write this letter to request that Lee Scott not be paroled. I saw the body of Dana Marie Weaver!

Rev. A. Wayne Schwab, the rector at St. Paul's Episcopal Church, Montvale NJ wrote to Mr. Charles P. Chew, Director of the Parole Board, on June 13, 1961

I write in behalf of Lee Scott who has been a prisoner for the last twelve years in the State prison at Richmond in hopes that he might be granted a conditional release from prison.

I do not know Lee personally but was assistant minister at his family's church in Washington D.C. from 1954 to 1956. There I came to know his father and daughter. This gave me a 'kind' of direct contact with Lee. I picked up general impressions of him from parishioners to the effect that the girl's death was more tragedy than pre-meditated action. The exact truth of course a jury has decided as best they can. What counts is that even then people did not believe

Lee to be sinister or criminal by nature. For this reason, I dare to write to you in his behalf.

If I can be of any help, I shall be only too glad to do so.

Dr. George S. Hurt, a doctor of obstetrics and gynecology with offices in Roanoke VA typed a letter to Mr. Charles P. Chew, Director of the Parole Board, on June 13, 1961

I noticed in the paper that Lee Scott is coming up for parole.

As I think back on his condition and actions which lead [sic] up to the crime for which he was committed, I feel that it would be extremely dangerous for him to be turned loose at this time, or at any time without having a thorough psychiatric work out.

His background is certainly not one that would make one feel at all certain as to his rehabilitation.

Mrs. Maynard F. Arthur, living in Roanoke VA wrote to the Hon. L. Almond, Governor of Virginia, on June 13, 1961

In regard to a pardon for "Buddy" Scott, we (my husband & I) are "opposed" for he did a violent, cruel murder and he deserves more time than twelve (12) years. He was sentenced for life, he has never had to do hard labor and to turn him loose (at 28 years of age) is inviting him to do more violence. We pardon too many criminals and in a short time, they commit another act of violence. I hope you will consider and review his case thoroughly for he really was a bad boy.

William E. Gilbert, who recently was the mayor of the City of Radford VA typed a letter (on city letterhead stationery) to the Honorable Committee on Pardons and Parole for the Virginia State Penitentiary on June 15, 1961

> Some days ago, there was a news item in the Roanoke Times about releasing Prisoner Scott who murdered a girl in a church in Roanoke city some 12 years ago.

> I am not related or acquainted even with any of the families involved in this matter; but do feel that if this man is allowed to get out of prison in such a short time, the example will be bad for society. Justice would not be done in as full a measure as it should be.

> This is not a gracious position for me to take, but somebody must speak up for holding the line; and letting your committee know the public is concerned.

> My term as Mayor closed Sept. 1, 1960, so I am just a private citizen now.

Miss Bertha W. Starritt, living in Roanoke VA wrote a letter to the Chairman Parole Board on June 15, 1961

> I wish to register my protest against the movement to parole one, Lee Scott, from a 99 years sentence for the crime he committed several years ago. What do the terms – law and justice – mean these days? At the time of that murder, I was associated closely with the victims of the tragedy, as I was principal of Crystal Spring School, Roanoke City, of which Mrs. Dana Weaver, the mother of the murdered girl, was secretary. I never shall forget those trying days, and my heart and mind cry out against any move that would shorten the prison term of the perpetrator. One has to be close to a scene of this type to fully realize the enormity of the crime, and the suffering it entails—suffering as long as life lasts!

What does the future hold for us, if the arm of the law and the scales of justice hand us nothing but, "Murderer, go free!" I pray that you and members of your Board will decide to drop this movement to parole Lee Scott. Not only may the present suffer as a result of his freedom now, but the future may reap a whirlwind of crime because of this leniency! Let's stand for law and order – not leniency! Yes, I believe in being charitable, but I prefer safety when dealing with one who may not have learned this lesson, even yet.

Thelma Loyd (Mrs. A. Tracy Loyd) residing in Roanoke VA used the letterhead stationery of the Virginia State Association of the National Association of Parliamentarians, Inc. when she wrote a letter to Mr. Charles P. Chew, Director of the Parole Board, on June 15, 1961

> While on vacation, I heard that Scott—the murderer of Dana Marie Weaver—is to appear before the Parole Board for release from prison.
>
> We who live in Roanoke remember him as a very sadistic, arrogant and very unpleasant sort of person in every respect, even as a small boy.
>
> Please do not release this man on a defenseless society. The citizens of Roanoke are really up in arms at the very thought of such a thing.
>
> We beg of you – do not release this man.

Rev. J. Paul Gruver, D.D., a minister at the First Evangelical United Brethen Church, Roanoke VA typed a letter to Mr. Charles P. Chew, Director of the Parole Board, on June 16, 1961

> I am concerned for the possible parole of Mr. Lee Scott.
>
> I have known Mrs. Dana Weaver for more than twenty years and am concerned for her just now in the possible parole of the one who killed her daughter, Dana Marie.

Surely the mother should have every assurance that the one guilty of the act taking her daughter's life, is paroled only after the most careful consideration for Mrs. Weaver. What assurance can she be given that he has proven his right to a parole at the earliest time possible under the sentence? Does his record as a prisoner give evidence of genuine sorrow that he took the life of a young girl who had such a promising future? If Mr. Scott is returned to society without a great change in his character and personality, this will add to the burden carried so well by Mrs. Weaver over these years.

I often wonder if Mr. Scott ever made any attempt to communicate with Mrs. Weaver, in which he revealed the tragedy in his own life by what he caused in their lives?

I know only faintly your heavy responsibility and ask only for what is best not alone for Mrs. Weaver but for the larger community in which we all live.

Mr. and Mrs. Clifford R. Mehnert, living in Roanoke VA typed a letter to Mr. Charles P. Chew, Director of the Parole Board, on June 16, 1961

Recently it was announced on television that Lee Scott would appear before your board soon for parole.

That tragedy will never be forgotten here in Roanoke, and as citizens of Roanoke for the past fifty years, we are asking you not to release that sick mind to do the same thing over again.

If the victim had been our daughter, we would never want him to be released.

Letters from Concerned Citizens, Relatives of the Victim, or Friends of the Prisoner, Addressed to the Governor of Virginia or to the Members of the Parole Board, Preserved in the Governor's Executive Papers, Dated in the Fall of 1965

Lee Goode Scott's aunt Mrs. Julia Rasche, living in Cincinnati OH wrote a several letters to the governor's office in 1965, a few of which are preserved in the executive records. On June 30, 1965, she wrote a letter to Martha Bell Conway, Secretary of the Commonwealth of Virginia, to say:

> Last week, when I was in Richmond, you spent your valuable time discussing with me over the telephone the case of my nephew, Lee Goode Scott, 57143, Virginia State Penitentiary.
>
> This is to tell you that I am very grateful to you for your kindness in giving me your time in discussing the matter with me.
>
> We all hope that the Parole Board will make a favorable decision for us soon, so that we may have Lee with us at home.
>
> Thank you very much.

On November 15, 1965, Mrs. Rasche typed a letter to Martha Bell Conway, Secretary of the Commonwealth of Virginia, to say:

> In June of this year I made a trip to Richmond to talk to the Parole Board in regard to my nephew, Lee Scott, #57143. While I was there you were kind enough to discuss the case with me by telephone. During that talk you stated that you could neither act yourself nor advise me until the Parole Board reached a decision.

On September 27 parole was denied. In the meantime Lee had been given the privilege of working outside. Thus he has had a time to become acclimated to the outside world as it now is.

I was wondering if at this time you would feel free to say anything regarding this matter. It seems to me that it would be a good time to ask for parole before Governor Harrison leaves the office, but knowing so little about such matters, I hesitate to write directly to him without advice from someone who knows.

Also, some friends have said they would like to write to Governor Harrison in Lee's behalf, but would it not be better for them to write directly to the Parole Board?

Thank you very much for any help you may give me regarding this matter.

On November 28, 1965, Mrs. Rasche typed a letter to Albertis S. Harrison Jr. the Honorable Governor of Virginia, to say:

It is my understanding that you are at present considering the matter of a pardon for Lee Scott, #57143.

In connection with this I would like to point out that on previous occasions I have offered a home to Lee with my family at the above address, for as long as he desires.

Also, when I talked with the parole board last June I pointed out that there were several jobs available to him. At present I would like to tell you that Brigadier Maude A. McGowan of the Salvation Army and also the administrator of William Booth Memorial Hospital of Covington, Kentucky, has stated that she would give Lee work at the hospital at any time when he would be in a position to accept it.

Booth Hospital is also my place of employment. Although it has a Kentucky address it is only across the Ohio River from Cincinnati, thus very convenient for commuting.

With this work, and with the help of Brigadier McGowan and the other Salvation Army officers, I feel sure that we would be able to assist Lee in making the adjustments necessary.

Thank you very much for your kind attention to this matter.

THESE ADDITIONAL LETTERS dating from the last couple of months in Gov. Harrison's term were preserved in the executive records.

Mrs. Laurence G. Hoes (the wife of the man who founded the James Monroe Memorial Library), residing in Washington DC, typed a letter to Albertis S. Harrison Jr. the Honorable Governor of Virginia on October 15, 1965.

I am hoping you will remember me in connection with the James Monroe Memorial Library in Fredericksburg.

I am taking the liberty of writing you in behalf of a young man who has been a prisoner in the State Penitentiary for sixteen years.

His name is Lee Goode Scott and he was convicted of first degree murder in connection with the death of a girl in Roanoke in May 1949. I knew his mother, a gentle little lady whose heart was broken over the tragedy and who died a year or so later.

Lee has maintained from the first that he did not intend to commit the crime and it was brought out in the trial that it was not premeditated, which the circumstances certainly bore out. He had hardly ever seen the girl in his life and only met at their church by chance, both thinking that a meeting was to be held there. While waiting, they had an argument when she belittled his hero, a football player. He spoke sharply and she struck out at him with a pop bottle. In the ensuing struggle, the girl was suffocated.

I will go no farther into the details, since these are available to you. Suffice it to say that no motive was uncovered and absolutely no sex angle. However, the hue and cry in Roanoke engulfed the boy and his whole family - so much so that his mother, father and little sister had to leave Roanoke because of threats against the little girl's life in retaliation.

He has been a model prisoner. I have seen him several times, as has my husband, and have corresponded with him over the years. There has never been a trace of bitterness. He has pulled himself up by his own bootstraps, admits he had to be punished, and has a lively, apparently healthy attitude toward the world in general. He has great artistic talent. His paintings of the eight Virginia presidents were on public display in Richmond several years ago, and he has painted for me a head of Christ which is breathtaking from a boy who has never had a lesson. He also made an amazing copy of the Rembrandt Peale portrait of James Monroe which is in the Monroe Library in Fredericksburg.

The parole board states it judges his case impartially and is subject to no influence; yet each time the boy's case comes up, they are bombarded from Roanoke by bitter, vitriolic letters threatening all sorts of things if he should be released. The Roanoke Times-World News is particularly vindictive, reprinting Lee's picture and all the details each time he comes up for parole.

A number of clergymen and many others have felt from the first that Lee's sentence should have been for manslaughter, not murder. Yet here he has served sixteen years in prison with no apparent hope of release. I myself have been very much impressed with Lee's progress in educating himself. His letters are beautifully written and show thought. I wish so very much he could be given a chance, but, as I see it, you are his only hope as long as people in Roanoke continue their barrage of objections to his release.

I hope you will understand my object in writing you. I feel so keenly that this is a waste of good human material and that something can be made of this man.

MARTHA BELL CONWAY personally drafted a reply to Mrs. Hoes on October 18, 1965, saying, "Your husband was in the office a week or so ago requesting an appointment with the Governor. In discussing this matter with the Governor, he expressed a wish to see the father of Lee Scott, and has an appointment with him this week."

Mr. B.E. Estes, Attorney at Law, with offices in Roanoke VA typed a letter to Gov. Albertis S. Harrison on November 10, 1965.

I would like to be among those suggesting to you that some relief is in order for the above party. I have personally known the family for some years even prior to the tragedy. In fact, as a Citizenship Merit Badge Counselor, I had helped Buddy with his Boy Scout work.

It is my thought that the opposition to Buddy would materially lessen if such parties knew that he would not return to Roanoke as a resident. Personally, I feel that he would not return here.

I sincerely hope that he may receive your favorable consideration.

Hon. Kermit V. Rooke, Judge, Juvenile and Domestic Relations Court, Richmond VA typed a brief letter to Gov. Albertis S. Harrison on November 17, 1965

My attention has been directed to the fact that consideration will probably be given to granting a conditional pardon to Lee G. Scott, currently a prisoner in the State Penitentiary.

I would like for you to know that I have become quite well acquainted with this young man and have been impressed that he has potentiality for constructive citizenship. Should it be your decision to grant him a pardon, it would be my intention to cooperate closely in rendering every possible assistance to the young man, to the end that he may become established in our community and not be a burden to society.

The husband of Lee Goode Scott's paternal aunt, Mr. F.E. McNeace, Sr. living in Roanoke VA typed a brief letter to Gov. Albertis S. Harrison. The letter is not dated but is recorded by the governor's office as received prior to November 19, 1965.

In our era of human rights and concern, I pause a few minutes to bring to your attention the plight of Lee G. Scott of Roanoke, Virginia, who at the age of sixteen years received from the local jury the verdict of first degree murder, rather than involuntary manslaughter. Scott is now thirty-two years old and his record while confined these past sixteen years has been just as exemplary as was his life before this tragic accident.

I believe that I speak for a number of Roanoke citizens when I ask for your clemency in behalf of Lee Scott. It is tragic—that he is still an inmate at the prison in Richmond. I urge that he be pardoned and allowed to assume responsibilities in the work-a-day world which he is well qualified to do.

With your help may compassion prevail for Lee Scott.

Lee Goode Scott's cousin Mr. Charles Bruce McNeace, living in Louisville KY typed a brief letter to Gov. Albertis S. Harrison on November 18, 1965.

As an agent and operator for the Chesapeake and Ohio Railway Company, and as a former citizen of Roanoke, I have followed the plight of Lee Scott through these seventeen years. I should like to be counted among those who believe that Lee Scott has over paid a debt to society. This young man, I understand, has borne his long punishment well, and is eligible for pardon or parole.

My family and I beg of you, our Governor, to exercise your power of authority and pardon this young man so that he may be allowed to assume his responsibilities in the every-day way of life.

With your help may compassion prevail for Lee Scott.

Mr. Edmund W. Burruss, living in Roanoke VA typed a letter to Gov. Harrison on November 12, 1965.

I am writing you on behalf of Lee Scott who has been a prisoner in the State Penitentiary since 1949. He was convicted of the murder of Dana Marie Weaver which occurred in the kitchen of Christ Episcopal Church on May 8, 1949 in Roanoke.

I knew Lee Scott from the time he was a baby as he lived on our street. Prior to this tragic occurrence he was regarded as a very good boy by all who knew him. He was very active in Christ Episcopal Church and was an Eagle Scout. He was loyal to his parents and popular among his friends.

He has been in the penitentiary for 16 years which is half of his life as he was only a 16 year old boy when he was committed to prison. I understand that he has been a model prisoner and I believe he should be given his freedom in order to prove himself a useful member of society. Anything you can do on behalf of Lee Scott, toward granting him a parole or pardon, will be greatly appreciated by his family and friends.

Mr. Joseph Forman, living in Roanoke VA typed a letter to Gov. Harrison on November 9, 1965.

This boy, during his younger years, was my neighbor. He enjoyed a superb reputation up to the time of an unaccountable lapse of a few moments duration.

Your fellow Virginian of seventy years thinks Lee Scott is a subject of forgiveness. I hope in the coming seasons of Thanksgiving and Christmas you will find time to give this boy, now man, a chance to rehabilitate himself with a conditional pardon.

Mr. Frank Sink, living in Roanoke VA typed a letter to Gov. Harrison on November 13, 1965.

I am writing to you concerning Lee Scott.

I have known Lee for many years. We were in high school together when the tragedy in which he was involved occurred. Since that time I have constantly written to him and have traveled to Richmond to visit and encourage him several times when the Warden has given me special permission to do so.

This effort on my part has been sustained because I have a strong belief In Lee. I knew Lee's achievements prior to the tragedy and I have kept informed of his accomplishments while he has been in prison. It is for these reasons that I feel justified to convey to you my strong belief that if restored to a free life, Lee will make a useful and responsible citizen.

For myself, I would urge you that I believe that the Roanoke Times and World News has indeed wielded its power much too long in this case!

With appreciation for your untiring efforts in the office which you hold, I am, Yours Sincerely

Mr. Walter P. Smith Jr. living in Sandston VA typed a letter to Gov. Harrison on November 16, 1965.

At the request of Mr. Norman G. Scott I am writing concerning his son Lee Scotts 57143, TQ12 State Penitentiary.

On numerous occasions I have met and talked with Lee, and having a reasonable knowledge of his background, it is my honest opinion that Lee can join our society and become a useful and productive citizen.

I am in complete accord with any action to conditionally pardon this man. At one time I had arranged for a position for him as well as a place of worship and residence, anticipating action in his favor of the state parole board. He has the endorsement of many members of the Robert E. Lee Council Boy Scout Executive Board, as well as other outstanding citizens. If the authorities should require that Lee reside in Richmond, he will have our full cooperation and assistance.

Please notify me if there is any way I can be of service to you in the future.

Mr. Melvin S. Ruffner, living in New York City, typed a brief letter to Gov. Harrison on November 18, 1965.

May I take this opportunity to strongly recommend that a conditional pardon be granted to Mr. Lee Scott.

I have been corresponding with Lee for 15 years and find him most worthy to become a useful citizen and well deserving of such a pardon.

I earnestly trust that your review of the facts including his model prison record, coupled with the recommendations of the responsible State Officials, and private individuals like myself, will influence a favorable decision.

Professor Roy L. Garis, at Pepperdine College, Los Angeles CA typed a letter to Gov. Harrison on November 22, 1965

I am a native Virginian and was Assistant Commissioner of Public Welfare in Tennessee for two years and had the entire state institutions under my jurisdiction. In this connection I became well aware of many of the problems faced by the men in the penitentiary.

I am writing to you in behalf of one of your present inmates, Lee Scott (#57143 TQ12). You have a letter in the files of the Parole Board which I wrote in his behalf about April 15, 1961. I trust that you will have your secretary recover this letter from your files and read it into his present record. The things I advised at that time have been well substantiated in Lee's behalf since then. I think he is well deserving of a conditional parole at this time, and trust that you will grant it to him while you are in office. I could submit to you much more information, but there is very little I can add to what I have already stated to the Governor of Virginia in my letter of April 15th. As a matter of justice to this young man, I trust you will look upon him with favor at this time.

Rev. C. Julian Bartlett, Dean of Grace Cathedral, San Francisco CA typed a two-page letter to Gov. Harrison on November 23, 1965

During the years 1950 through 1955, I was Rector of St. Paul's Episcopal Church, Rock Creek Church Road, Washington D. C. During that time, I numbered among my congregation the family of Mr. Norman Garrett Scott. You will recall that Mr. Scott is the father of Lee Scott, now serving a sentence of Life Imprisonment at #500 Spring Street, Richmond.

During my tenure at St. Paul's, Washington, I counted the Scotts among my friends and had the opportunity to minister to them through trying years. Their son Lee had begun his term in prison just several years before my arrival in Washington. I had occasion during those five years to make trips to Richmond to see Lee, and kept in touch with both him and the Chaplain at the Penitentiary. I was with Mr. Scott during the night when Mrs. Scott died. So, you see that I was close to them. Since coming to San Francisco in 1956, I have continued to correspond with Lee from time to time.

Every word I ever received about Lee during the five years I was in Washington, indicated that his record at the Penitentiary was outstandingly good. I have continued to be amazed by the maturity he has shown through the years. Never have I heard him express bitterness or rebelliousness. The details of his record I am sure speak for themselves.

I understand that Lee has applied for a pardon and that there is a possibility that he could be granted a "Conditional Pardon". As you know, he entered the Penitentiary as a teenaged boy. He is now a grown man. Without question, he has paid a substantial price for the crime of which he was convicted.

I do not wish to be presumptuous by offering advice regarding aspects of this matter in which I am not competent. However, I have assumed that you would welcome this testimony from one who has served as Lee's Pastor in the past and from one who has known the deep tragedy and suffering which has been sustained by Lee's family through these many years. If you wish to send any inquiries to me concerning this matter, I shall be eager to be as cooperative as possible.

Mr. Webster T. Stone, living in Roanoke VA typed a letter to Gov. Harrison on December 3, 1965.

Having dealt with young people all of my life, I am, now, writing you concerning one whom I would like very much to help. The one whom I have reference to is Lee Scott.

I understand that he is being considered for conditional parole at this time, and I do hope that you can look upon this decision favorably.

This young man was a member of my wife's Sixth Grade class at Highland Park Elementary School and in my class at Lee Jr. High School in Roanoke, Virginia. We found Lee a very cooperative student and never had an occasion to question his reliability or moral standards. He was active in Scout work and Young Peoples' work at Christ Episcopal Church here.

I knew his family as patrons of the school and in business. I bought an insurance policy from Mr. Scott.

Perhaps you are wondering who I am. I am Webster T. Stone, one of the Brunswick County Stones, and a brother of Mrs. Mattie S. Bishop. I taught in Lee Jr. High School in Roanoke for twenty-eight years until my retirement.

Trusting that my request is reasonable in your judgment and that you will give this young man a chance to become a rehabilitated citizen of Virginia which he, in my opinion, deserves.

The dentist Dr. Daniel R. Miller, living in St. Petersburg FL typed a letter to Gov. Harrison on December 17, 1965. He used a fashionable electric typewriter that produced a cursive script typeface, long before the days of computerized word processing where italics can be created/toggled at the touch of a button.

I am writing to you today to speak on behalf of Lee Scott in the sincere hope that he may be granted a conditional pardon. I don't believe it is necessary to delve into the accidental and unintentional nature of this sad tragedy because I know you are acquainted with those facts.

I have kept in touch with Lee over the years and have seen how he has become a good Christian and has rehabilitated himself into a good and worthwhile person. In fact, I was able to visit him this December 12th and leave him some articles for Christmas; although I hope and pray that he will get a much nicer Christmas present!

He deserves the chance to become part of the world again. I enter this plea for Lee Scott with complete faith in the goodness and worth that is in him. I thank you for the opportunity to tell about my belief in Lee.

I pray you will take this letter to heart and give Lee the blessed gift of freedom.

Also, if necessary, I can find him a job here in St. Petersburg when he is released.

Rev. Joseph Tatnall, Director of the North Arlington Child Care Centers, Inc. in Arlington VA typed a letter to Gov. Harrison on December 7, 1965.

Over the past nine years I have been the pastor and spiritual advisor to Lee G. Scott. I first learned of this sixteen year old boy's tragedy from his father who was a member of my congregation in Washington, D.C., and how that a sentence of first degree murder was given to Lee when the actual facts of the case pointed to involuntary manslaughter.

This exceptional young man (he is now thirty-two years old) does not need a character reference from me at this time. His record both before and after imprisonment speaks for itself. I have visited with him a number of times, and have exchanged a letter every month. I am acutely aware of his maximum readiness now for rehabilitation in the workaday world. He has been denied parole five or six successive times and I would hope that he has not been singled out for a future of wasted and embittered years.

Lee Scott is a superior individual with many natural talents. He needs to begin college training and to support himself with either a part-time or full-time job of which there are several waiting for him in Washington. Five good homes, as well as his own father's, are ready to receive him as a member of the family and to help him adjust to community life.

Therefore, I hope that you will use the mercy of your office to the fullest and grant to Lee Scott full pardon; however, if there must needs be a parole plan, I would count it a privilege to cooperate with you in every way possible.

May God's love, shown as at this time in the birth of Jesus, be available for Lee Scott in a new Year of hope and opportunity for life and work.

With every good wish and seasonal greetings, I am Gratefully yours,

Rev. E. Pinkney Wroth, rector of St. Paul's Episcopal Church, Rock Creek Church Rd. Washington DC typed a letter to Gov. Harrison on December 20, 1965.

As Rector of St. Paul's Episcopal Church, Rock Creek Parish in Washington, D. C., which for many years has carried Lee Scott (57143-TQ 12) as a member of the church, I am writing to urge action as soon as possible on his parole or pardon.

I have visited Lee on several occasions when I have been in Richmond, and on that basis alone, feel that he has the will and motivation as well as the Christian character, to make a successful readjustment to society. As I have indicated in times past, I stand willing to help him gain adequate employment upon his release.

I realize that you have heard from many sources on this matter and that sometimes you must feel like Pilate in wishing to be rid of the matter. I can only say I speak in behalf of all of our congregation who have known the Scott family for many years in saying that we are hopeful this matter will be resolved promptly.

AFTER LEE GOODE SCOTT'S release, there are only two more letters of reaction from the general community, preserved at the end of this collection of documents in the governor's executive papers.

Miss Bertha W. Starritt, living in Roanoke VA wrote a letter to Ex-Gov. Albertis S. Harrison on January 19, 1966.

Dear Sir: I wish to protest your conditional pardon of Lee Goode Scott. Conditional, yes, but one can "read between the line" here!

If you had "lived through" that horrible epoch in our city's history, I think you would never have granted Scott this freedom.

As a school principal at that time, the murdered girl's mother was my secretary, and I know all the details of that crime. What he – an animal in human form – did then, he may do again! Do you wish to be responsible for such a risk? I didn't know this boy, but I give him credit for not having planned this crime. I knew this lovely, innocent girl and her family.

The plea for pardon has come up more than once, and I have protested. And as a farewell act in your administration, you show this leniency!! The act doesn't go with your good record as Virginia's Governor. Think on these things!

Mr. John C. Page, living in Winston-Salem NC wrote a letter to the honorable Albertis S. Harrison on January 29, 1967.

The enclosed clipping concerns an incident that took place at the time of "Buddy" Scott's – what? Tragedy?

We may not know what to expect of him, ever, but I'll be glad to take my chances with him – a person who's made an effort to be responsible.

Perhaps the dreadful sacrifice of this little girl may be of some meaning to humans, some day.

Your action towards him *[text crossed out: renews the little faith I...]* moves me.

Chapter 13. Pardoning the 99-Year Sentence

THE GOVERNOR OF VIRGINIA from 1962 to 1966, Albertis S. Harrison Jr., had a background in the criminal justice system serving as the Commonwealth's Attorney for Brunswick County. He was also a member of the Virginia State Senate and the state's Attorney General just prior to his election as governor. During his tenure as governor, Harrison focused on industrial development and diversification, built new postsecondary technical schools, expanded branch colleges, modernized highways, and promoted tourism. After leaving office, he served on the Virginia Supreme Court and chaired the Commission on Constitutional Revision.

Meanwhile, Mr. Scott found a new ally in the U.S. Senator from Virginia, the influential Harry F. Byrd who is best known as the driving force behind the so-called Massive Resistance political movement that bitterly opposed desegregation and civil rights reforms. Through a series of letters and personal visits to the senator's office in Washington D.C., Mr. Scott moved Senator Byrd to write a letter to Gov. Harrison. There is an abundance of information about the power and influence of the Byrd Organization, as it was called. This Democratic political machine gained traction in the 1930s with opposition to President Roosevelt's New Deal and continued into the 1960s with resistance to President Kennedy's and President Johnson's progressive social programs. Senator Byrd had a particular influence in Virginia state politics. It was once said, "Governors of Virginia are appointed by Harry Byrd, subject to confirmation by the electorate... He ruled not with a command but with a nod." Ironically, this favor for Mr. Norman Garrett Scott would be one of the last acts of influence that Senator Byrd would perform. He retired from the Senate three months after drafting a letter to the Governor of Virginia on behalf of Lee Scott, and died of a brain tumor the following year.

When the letter from Senator Byrd, dated August 11, 1965, hit the desk of Gov. Harrison, he sat up and paid attention. The letter is addressed "My dear Albertis" and goes on to say, "My friend of long standing, Garrett Scott of Roanoke and Washington D.C., called to see me on yesterday in the interest of his son, Lee Scott, who has been serving a term in the penitentiary for 16 years." The senator includes two attachments, provided by Mr. Scott no doubt. One is a memorandum that lists Lee Scott's many outward accomplishments. Another is a letter of reference from the Boy Scouts of America which, as Senator Byrd describes it, "is highly complimentary of his efforts while he has been incarcerated." The letter ends politely. "I will thank you to advise me in order that I may make a report to my friend, Garrett Scott."

Harrison replied to Senator Byrd within a day. "This boy is eligible for parole consideration and I am advised by the State Parole Board that it is now reviewing the case. During my administration, a large file of correspondence has built up in regard to this young man and the offense in Roanoke. The slaying was widely publicized and strong sentiment apparently has persisted among some people in the Roanoke area against releasing Scott. However, I know the Parole Board will give impartial consideration to the case, including the information which Mr. Scott has supplied."

Lee Scott came to be interviewed by the Virginia Parole Board for a fifth time in the summer of 1965. As part of that process, a summary report was prepared; unfortunately the last page is missing, as mentioned in Chapter 11, and so the writer's identity is only known as the person who conducted Lee Scott's intake interview in 1949. The report remarks upon the youth's temperament at the time of his incarceration, "the sternness with which he met his conviction and sentence of ninety nine (99) years and the utter lack of expression in his eyes the day of the interview." He goes on to describe the changes that he observed in Lee Scott since that time. "I find that in sixteen (16) years this youth has grown into a rather personable person, able to smile, investigate more deeply himself and the necessary factors for successful living, and to appreciate what he has accomplished during the course of his imprisonment. Like I said in the outset, I have watched Lee Scott grow and have seen him defeat many of the problems that I, as his initial interviewer, felt surely would cause his downfall in prison."

This unnamed interviewer, in the same report, goes on at length to advocate for granting Lee Scott's parole. "Scott has appeared before the Parole Board a total of four (4) times and received 'turned down' on each occasion. Though he has no hostility toward the Parole Board for their action, he seems to feel that they are being governed by the Roanoke newspapers, who seem to persist in bringing his case to light on the slightest provocation." This person concluded his summary report with a recommendation, addressed to the Division of Corrections, "There are times in every man's conviction when, it is felt, they have reached that point of release and it then becomes a problem of letting them stay or turning them loose in hopes that the judgment of the releasing agent is correct. It is felt that Lee Scott has reached a point where he could be released. To continue punishment may well lead him to disregard the aims and goals he has worked for up to this point and revert to his old way of thinking."

Nevertheless, the three-man parole board issued their official decision to the governor's office in the first week of October. The decision is signed by Charles P. Chew, James W. Phillips, and Pleasant C. Shields and says, in part, "He has been interviewed and his case thoroughly studied on five different occasions. The most recent parole denial was recorded on September 27, 1965. His discharge date now is established as March 31, 2015." In other words, there was no hope but for Lee Scott to remain in prison for the next forty-nine years.

A rare gem—a letter written by Lee Scott himself—was uncovered among the governor's cache of records. This document was preserved courtesy of another notable Virginian: Laurence G. Hoes a great-great-grandson of President James Monroe and a founder of the James Monroe Museum and Memorial Library in Fredericksburg, Virginia. From a separate letter written by his wife, around the same time, it is revealed that they were close acquaintances with his parents for many years. Mrs. Hoes writes, "I knew his mother, a gentle little lady whose heart was broken over the tragedy and who died a year or so later."

On October 27, 1965, Mr. Hoes wrote to Governor Harrison, "I think that you may know that I am very interested in the case of Lee Scott who is an inmate of the penitentiary in Richmond for murder committed 17 years ago when he was 17. He has been up before the parole board 5 times without favorable results. I go in to see him when I am in Richmond so that he can feel that some person has a personal interest in him.... I am enclosing a letter which I received from Lee recently and it gives his opinion why he cannot receive favorable consideration, though a member of the parole board told me that outside pressure to keep him behind bars had <u>nothing to do with their</u>

<u>decision</u>…. It is my personal opinion that this case should be determined on the merits of his present situation rather than on the grounds of still remaining hatred for him in Roanoke. If this feeling in that city remains, Lee Scott will never be able to obtain his freedom and try to make something of himself in life after such a terrible start."

The letter that Mr. Hoes provided to the governor is dated October 18, 1965 in Lee Scott's handwriting, rubber-stamped with the approval of the penitentiary's censors. The faded mirror image of the back side of the page shows that the paper is a sheet of the printed rules for visitors. Interestingly, he writes in print letters not cursive.

"Dear Mr. Hoes, Whenever I see Mr. Smyth, he asks if I have heard any good news. If, by chance, there has been some, I tell him because this is his way of seeing how much information reaches through – and perhaps, he is gauging my outlook. Of course Mr. Smyth is in a position to know what is happening but last week there was nothing I could say regarding good news.

"However, Friday I talked with a former parole supervisor who later became rehabilitation officer and is now the asst. superintendent. The reason I listed some of Mr. Oliver's background is because he has known me a long time, is familiar with my case and qualified to speak about it. Well, I learned why he endorsed the recommendation for conditional pardon. He said it very simply and clearly. He said the parole board didn't want the responsibility of paroling me.

"Their position must be difficult to maintain and augment over the years. The newspaper pressure makes a favorable decision impossible for them but now they have criticism from both sides and from within their conscience because I fully meet their own standards and qualifications for parole. A conditional pardon would take the board off the hook. I would be released but freedom would be limited by the conditions and regulations of parole.

"It was a pleasure to see you earlier this month and I enjoyed our visit. Sincerely, Lee."

Among the governor's records is a single sheet of yellow notepad paper with handwritten notes, apparently from a staff meeting where the case was discussed. Dated October 21, 1965, here are the secretary's notes of that meeting—never before published—showing some of the governor's considerations on the issue. *Norman Garrett Scott in office with Governor... Mrs.*

Scott died of heart attack in 1952... Daughter is in Lowell, Mass. married... Real & insurance in Roanoke – from 1911... Man's sister lives there... Couldn't work in Roanoke for past 16 years... Massachusetts Protective Insurance... Sees Lee Scott 2 or 3 times a year... Sees sister in Roanoke 2 or 3 times a year... John Pratt, lawyer in Washington, tried to get transcript, but never got it... Knows attorney clientele in Roanoke... Can't ignore public sentiment—... Advise him to carefully seek out sentiment among the [unreadable] people in Roanoke, good record, made good adjustment.... Is he ready to return? Is society ready to accept him? Someday he will get out –only question is, "Is this the right time?"... Need letters from prominent people in Roanoke in file. Bring about a change of sentiment in Roanoke.

Governor Harrison, with his term coming to an end, had a number of clemency applications to decide before surrendering his seat to the next person. He dealt with a few others in fairly short order but saved the most controversial case for last.

Harrison signed Lee Scott's pardon on Friday, January 14, 1966, literally his last day in the office. The next governor was due to start his term on the following Monday.

Chapter 14. Starting Over as a Free Man

ON THURSDAY, JANUARY 13, 1966, Gov. Harrison issued an official Memorandum to the Parole Board. In a single typewritten paragraph, he changed Lee Goode Scott's life forever: "In view of his age (16) at the time of conviction, the length of time served with an excellent record, and upon the advice of penitentiary authorities that he has been rehabilitated to the fullest extent, I will grant this man a conditional pardon, provided a suitable plan for home and employment can be developed. He is to be under supervision for a period of five years, and if at any time during that five year period he violates the penal laws of the Commonwealth of Virginia, this pardon shall be null and void."

The Application for Conditional Pardon of Lee Goode Scott (prisoner number 57143) was granted, printed on official letterhead stationery, and signed by the governor the very next day. An official certificate was prepared, granting Lee Scott a conditional pardon effective January 14, 1966. He was not entirely free but would be "placed under the supervision of the Virginia Parole Board, subject to the rules, regulations, and conditions of parole as set forth in a parole agreement..." The terms would stay in place for five years until January 14, 1971, or unless he committed another offense.

No doubt, Lee's mind was buzzing with euphoria as he signed his name to the bottom of the declaration. This was his one and only chance to live outside the gray walls of the Virginia State Penitentiary and he grabbed it. If he had to abide by certain conditions and report to a parole officer for the next five years, that prospect seemed better than reporting minute-by-minute to guards at the jail.

There are essentially three categories of pardons in Virginia law. A simple pardon is a statement of forgiveness that, although it does not remove a conviction, it carries the benefit of a gold star-type of notation "pardon" on someone's record. An absolute pardon may be granted when the Governor is convinced that the petitioner is innocent of the charge for which he or she was convicted. The third type, a conditional pardon, is an act to modify or end a sentence imposed by the court. Conditional pardons are rare as the Governor does not typically substitute their judgment for that of the courts.

The governor's memo set one of the conditions that "a suitable plan for home and employment" had to be developed. An unsigned memo dated January 13, 1966, included with the records, summarized the plan for where Lee Scott would go to live upon his release. Printed here for the first time outside the governor's office, this informally handwritten memo explains the reasons why the ex-convict planned to go live in Ohio with his aunt.

"Mr. Peyton says: Re.: Lee Scott. Prefers to go to Aunt in Cincinnati, Ohio (mother's sister) – was with them frequently before – Uncle is living, gets along well with them, no connection between Aunt & Roanoke. Aunt has visited him and says he would have no difficulty in getting job as barber there but if he should then he could be employed temporarily in the hospital in which his aunt works as a physio-therapist. Worked in hospital (dental office) in pen. Aunt is 55 – Uncle is 57. One son (16). Good relation with cousin, frequently writes note on bottom of his mother's letter, although he has never seen him.

"Reason for preference – his sister is much younger and knows nothing of her activities and her marriage to Mr. Raymond Gauthier. They have young children and while sister is willing to help, he does not want to go with father because (1) too close to Va. & (2) father has new wife. Says there is plenty of work in Cincinnati."

Lee Scott walked out of the penitentiary's gates after sixteen years and six months behind bars. No longer the teenaged boy who entered with his hands in shackles, carrying only a New Testament and a hairbrush, now he was a thirty-three-year old man. His mother was long gone. His father had remarried and had a new wife.

Alone, he boarded a train in Richmond and travelled for several hours north to Cincinnati, Ohio. He settled into a new home with his aunt, his uncle, and a cousin who ironically at sixteen was exactly the same age that he had been when convicted of murder. Two weeks after getting out of prison, he typed a personal letter dated January 28, 1966 to Martha Bell Conway the Secretary of the Commonwealth, one of the government officials to co-sign his pardon certificate. He addressed the letter to Ms. Conway in friendly terms as a long-time acquaintance. This rare document describes his thoughts at the time and politely expresses his gratitude.

"Dear Miss Conway: My aunt made it a point to say that not everything in Richmond was discouraging last summer and she spoke of the encouragement she received in talking with you. Between summer and two weeks ago much has happened. At the Cincinnati depot Pat and Larry were waiting and drove me home. Winter has changed its appearance from that which I recall from spending youthful summers here. After almost seventeen years I am thankful and grateful to be with family and friends again. I will probably never know how much thanks are due you but I do want you to know that I appreciate everything you have done for me."

The documents in the governor's records have a nearly one year gap. By the end of that year and into the early part of 1967, the luster of freedom was apparently wearing off. As he acclimatized to life outside prison walls, it appears that Lee Scott began to feel the weight of his parole-like conditions. After twelve months, he celebrated his first Christmas holiday season in a family home. I imagine that he experienced a mixture of emotions while admiring the decorations on a Christmas tree sparkling in the light of a crackling fireplace. Everything felt, smelled, and tasted new. Familiar but strange.

Following that first Christmas on the outside, he began to wish for true freedom. He had a sampling of freedom, a re-kindling of sentiments from his lost childhood years. Perhaps he discovered one of the inconveniences of being a convicted felon on conditional release, that is, his basic rights as a U.S. citizen were under restrictions. He could not vote in the midterm elections held on November 8, 1966 during the middle of Democratic President Lyndon B. Johnson's second term. The Vietnam War was increasingly unpopular. Johnson's Democrats lost forty-seven seats to Republicans in the House of Representatives and three seats in the U.S. Senate. Despite the losses, the Democratic Party retained control of both chambers of Congress. Republicans won a large victory in the gubernatorial elections with a net gain of seven seats. This was the first election held after the passage of the Voting Rights Act of 1965, which led to a surge in African-American voter participation.

On December 29, 1966, Lee Scott wrote another brief letter to Martha Bell Conway. This time, instead of a typewriter he used a blue ballpoint pen. He continued using his style of printed letters, not cursive, and his handwriting shows characteristics of being narrow, tight, and slanted. Only his signature uses cursive.

"Dear Miss Conway: The sheer volume of work and variety of detail that flows across your desk astounds anyone who has seen the mail pour into your office. Having seen the mail delivery and even helped bring some of it while on pre-release training at the penitentiary, I have a small idea of the extent of the numerous jobs you are called upon to do. Also knowing of your personal and official interest in pardon cases, I am writing for any general information you can give regarding full pardons. Will you tell me what procedure should be followed? And, if it is permitted, can you guide me by saying what common pitfalls should be avoided? Best wishes for a happy new year!"

To her credit, Ms. Conway responded very promptly. In a letter dated January 4, 1967, she summarized the three types of pardons available in Virginia law: (1) absolute pardon, (2) a conditional pardon, and (3) a pardon without conditions. She explained, "You have a pardon of the second type and were placed under supervision. This pardon did not restore your civil rights, such as the right to hold office, vote, etc. When you have completed your period of supervision in a satisfactory manner, then you may apply to the Governor for removal of your political disabilities."

Just one week later, on January 10, 1967, Lee Scott sent another letter to Ms. Conway. Once again, he did not use a typewriter but instead penned his questions in blue ink, in his characteristic printing (not cursive) style.

"Dear Miss Conway: Thank you very much for your response to my request for information. It is helpful to know that there are three types of pardons available for the Governor's use. Would you tell me if it is possible to receive a pardon without conditions after one has been granted a conditional pardon? I wouldn't want to ask for the impossible. You said that when I have completed my period of supervision in a satisfactory manner then I could apply to the Governor for removal of my political disabilities. Could this period of supervision be removed or the length of time under these handicapping conditions be reduced by the Governor? Of course I would appreciate knowledge of how to go about applying for a type of executive clemency that would benefit me."

Ten days later, Ms. Conway replied in a brief typewritten letter dated January 20, 1967. She explained his situation in just two sentences: "After granting a pardon, it is most unusual for the Governor to change the conditions of the pardon. He has the authority to change the conditions, but exercises this authority only for the most pressing reasons." In other words, the answer was definitely no.

The records of the governor's office come to an end at this point. What happened to Lee Scott in the years to follow is speculation. Clearly the world had changed since he went "inside" and, like the world of the late 1960s compared to the late 1940s, he was no longer the same person. The last eighteen years of his life might have felt like a bad dream that he was awakening from. Whether or not he managed to get his conditions removed, by yet another in a series of Virginia's governors, his pardon's term was due to end in January 1971. At that point, it was close to twenty-two years since the day he went to the parish house for a game of ping-pong and ended up killing a girl in a spontaneous burst of rage.

It appears that once he was truly free of all restrictions, he wanted nothing more than to be reborn a new man and start his life over. His viewpoint echoed an anonymous rhyme etched into the walls of a prison cell. The Richmond-Times Dispatch published a retrospective article on their website titled *"From the Archives – the old Virginia State Penitentiary"* on September 11, 2022, with a series of photographs taken shortly before the facilities were demolished. Among the black-and-white images of cement walls and guard towers was the view of a small cell with a sink and a toilet. On the wall, someone had written:

> *When you enter here*
> *What you see here*
> *What you say here*
> *What you do here*
> *When you leave here*
> *Let it stay here*

After prison, he dreamed of making a living in the outside world as a barber. Why did this occupation appeal to him? I only have a snippet in Lee Scott's own words, quoted in the report submitted on June 22, 1965 to the parole board. "You don't have to explain too much about your past while you're cutting hair, where if you work in an office, there are always groups and cliques who seem to revel in the opportunity to bring up a fellow employee's background."

The short chapter in Nelson Harris's book *Hidden History of Roanoke* ends with a brief couple of sentences about what happened in Lee Scott's life after emerging from jail. "He left Virginia and moved west, married, raised a family and led a seemingly productive life. He died in the mid-1990s." But there is so much more to the story of the last thirty years of his life.

A friend of the Scott family declined to be interviewed for this project. He would only share that Lee Scott never spoke about the past. His children did not find out about what happened in Roanoke until just a few years ago. In uncovering this story after their father passed away, they felt extremely shocked. The website Find-A-Grave is a cemetery database that displays virtual memorials for over 200 million individuals. Lee Scott's memorial page shows him as a very average-looking, elderly man in a blue plaid shirt. He smiles for the camera while seated at a desk—a snapshot that captured one brief moment in an ordinary day.

Understandably, his children may not have discovered any of it without the invention of the internet, genealogy research websites, and historical newspapers becoming available online. Before the digital age, one had to physically travel to the public library and crank through reels of microfilm or pick through dusty stacks of yellowing newspaper pages. Until very recently, it was not easy to discover even the widely publicized details of someone's personal history.

I don't presume to understand how it feels to discover a scandal about a close member of the family. However, from making a thoughtful study of all the available materials surrounding this case, I have an inkling of why Lee Scott chose to focus on the joys of the present moment. When the prison gates rattled shut behind him for the last time, he compartmentalized that part of his youth and left it behind. He became a new person, joined a Lutheran church, and lived out a quiet life on a farm in Indiana. He died relatively young in the mid-1990s at the age of 63. Perhaps he often thought of St. Paul's words recorded in the New Testament, in Philippians 3:13-14, *Forgetting what is behind and straining toward what is ahead, I press on toward the goal to win the prize for which God has called me heavenward in Christ Jesus.* It is not at all surprising that he wished to leave this world surrounding by the loving smiles of a happy family; he gladly carried to the grave all the secrets of his shameful deed.

Epilogue. Finding Peace with the Past

"TO THOSE OF US WHO care, we need no reminder and to others it does not matter." These words, written by Dana Marie's mother in June 1961 in a letter to the governor of Virginia, have stuck in my mind as I reflect upon what I have learned in writing this book. As an outsider who grew up elsewhere, I never heard of this incident until Laurie Platt approached me to suggest a collaboration. Mrs. Weaver saw this crime and Lee's punishment as a family matter that should only concern those directly involved. Respectfully, I believe she was wrong about that. Everyone can learn from mistakes of the past—their own and the mistakes of others. Everyone who hears this story can take away valuable lessons about grief, trauma, shame, condemnation, rehabilitation, and forgiveness.

Yet, I feel that I've come to understand Mrs. Weaver's sentiment. Her voice has come across six decades of time to speak to me today. I've learned that Roanoke, Virginia is technically a city, with its history as a major railway depot and industrial center for the region, and still it has a small town feel. Everybody in the neighborhood knows everybody. Many families have generational roots in the streets and city parks; their names resonate in the surrounding counties. The natural rhythm of the mountains and valleys pulse in the flesh and blood of those who live there.

At Lee Scott's murder trial, the prosecutor and defense attorney, judge and jury pool, accused killer's family and the victim's grieving family... all of them knew each other. They grew up playing in each other's back yards, attended the same schools, enjoyed the same summertime barbeques, and sang the same Christmas carols on cold winter evenings. This was not merely a murder trial. This was a family drama, a betrayal of "one of our own" played out in the glaring spotlight of national media.

Even without 24-hour cable news television and social media, the newspapers managed to keep the sensational case alive in everyone's thoughts for years. Other publications picked up the story and scrambled to make a quick buck. A newspaper advertisement printed in *The Recorder* on September 30, 1949 excitedly announced the upcoming October issue of <u>Crime Detective</u> magazine, "...featuring the Dana Marie Weaver murder case which shocked Virginia some months ago when Dana Marie was murdered in a Church Parish house in Roanoke. For all the facts get a copy of this famous magazine at Valley News Store in Staunton, Virginia." The story was rehashed in a few other pulp fiction detective magazines over the next few years. A 1950s issue of the pulp magazine <u>Inside Detective</u> ran a tabloid style rendition of the story titled "Flesh and the Devil in the Parish House: The pretty, blonde girl fought her attacker tooth and nail—all to no avail. She died the horrible death of the martyred." The more the story circulated from one 15-cent magazine to the next, the more details got distorted and exaggerated. Accuracy in reporting was sacrificed for dialing up the entertainment value. If there were a Netflix back then, it's no doubt there would be a lurid documentary film.

In the traditional culture of Colonial Virginia, a family's name and reputation were a more valuable commodity than the land owned by an inherited estate, more precious than all the money in the bank. As a group, the whole town felt grief and shock, the violation of a sense of safety, that a "good boy" did something so terrible to a "good girl" in a good part of town—in the kitchen of a church no less. A girl should feel safe on the hallowed ground of a church. More than all that, the people must have worried that the town's name itself was forever tarnished. At the time, and perhaps even now, the citizens surely felt that Roanoke might be perceived by outsiders as one of "those places" where bad things happen. Their worst nightmares involved the side-eyes, the disapproving and judgmental stares of outsiders. But the truth is in a gray area somewhere in between. All of us are human beings. All of us harbor a dark streak inside. Anyone is capable of being triggered into a reckless, violent act under certain circumstances. It is a mistake to ignore this truth of human nature and pretend everything is "fine" when it is not.

SIX MONTHS AFTER DANA Marie's murder, on November 23, 1949, the mayor of Roanoke flipped a switch atop Mill Mountain to illuminate an

FLOWERS FOR DANA: THE 1949 MURDER OF DANA MARIE WEAVER IN THE "STAR CITY" ROANOKE, VIRGINIA

enormous neon-lit star. Originally, it was constructed as a seasonal Christmas decoration through sponsorship from the Roanoke Merchants Association. The plan was to dismantle the star when the holiday season ended. Obviously, those plans changed. The structure is eighty-eight feet tall, formed by two thousand feet of neon tubing mounted on a frame resembling a radio tower, and is actually three stars nested within each other. It is the largest, free-standing, man-made neon star in the world and one of the most popularly photographed attractions in the area. Most often it is pure white but the colors can be altered to red, white and blue on certain occasions, such as on the Fourth of July, to demonstrate the community's patriotism. The Roanoke Star is an iconic symbol, illuminated every night, to serve as a welcoming beacon to all.

After that first night, Roanoke earned the nickname "Star City of the South," and the star has remained part of the landscape of Mill Mountain ever since. Even on cloudy winter nights, the Roanoke Star brightly shines to remind us all that there is always a glimmer of hope to help us carry on to the next day. As former First Lady Eleanor Roosevelt once said, "It is better to light one small candle than to curse the darkness."

The End

Photographs

FIGURE 1. DANA MARIE Weaver's junior class portrait for the Jefferson High School yearbook, 1949 (Roanoke Public Library)

FIGURE 2. LEE GOODE Scott's junior class portrait for the Jefferson High School yearbook, 1949 (Roanoke Public Library)

FIGURE 3. PARISH HOUSE of Christ Episcopal Church, as viewed from Washington Street (photo by Laurie Platt)

FIGURE 4. ENTRANCE Door to the Parish House (photo by Laurie Platt)

FIGURE 5. UNNAMED RESIDENTS of Roanoke, VA participating in the scrap collection drive, circa October 1942 (Library of Congress)

FIGURE 6. UNNAMED RESIDENTS of Roanoke, VA participating in the kitchen fat collection drive with a visit to the local rendering plant, circa October 1942 (Library of Congress)

FIGURE 7. FAMILY SNAPSHOT of Lee Scott, as a seven year old child, with unidentified boy companion. This is one of two photographs submitted to the governor's office by the Scott family along with their pleadings for a pardon. (Library of Virginia)

FIGURE 8. FAMILY SNAPSHOT of Lee Scott as a child with his sister Judith, circa 1940. This is the second of two photographs submitted to the governor's office by the Scott family (Library of Virginia)

FIGURE 9. PRINCIPAL Payne with unnamed female students, from the 1949 Jefferson High School yearbook (Roanoke Public Library)

FIGURE 10. UNIDENTIFIED students in the hallways at Jefferson High School, from the 1949 yearbook (Roanoke Public Library)

FIGURE 11. SWIM CLASS at the high school, showing Lee Scott sitting on edge of pool at far left. From the 1949 Jefferson High School yearbook. (Roanoke Public Library)

FLOWERS FOR DANA: THE 1949 MURDER OF DANA MARIE WEAVER IN THE "STAR CITY" ROANOKE, VIRGINIA

FIGURE 12. LEE SCOTT, center, his face scratched, is led to a jail cell in Roanoke, Va., May 10, 1949, after Detective Frank H. Webb, glasses, announced that Scott had been charged with the church kitchen murder of Dana Marie Weaver, Scott's 16-year-old schoolmate. Scott, 16, is an Eagle Scout and a member of the church choir. Other officers are Sgt. Edgar Winstead, left, and Det. Jack Mitchell. Police received reports that Scott's face was scratched and they took him from his Jefferson High School class in Roanoke. (AP Photo/WF)

FIGURE 13. THE DETECTIVE Division of Roanoke City Police Department gives an interview to WSLS, WDBJ, and WROV radio stations in connection w/ investigation. Contributor: Roanoke City Police Department, 1949 (Roanoke Public Library)

FIGURE 14. CEMETERY headstone for the Weaver and Wimmer families' plot at Evergreen Burial Park in Roanoke (photo by Laurie Platt)

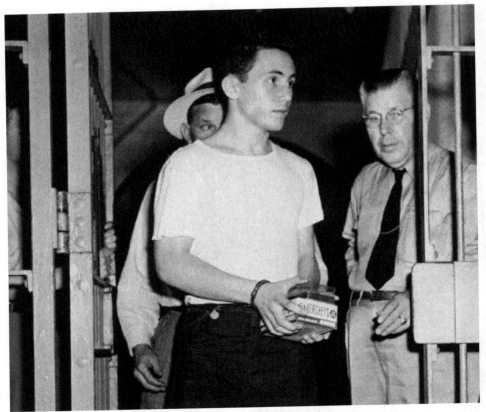

FIGURE 15. LEE SCOTT, 16, arrives at Virginia State Penitentiary in Richmond, to start his 99-year sentence for slaying classmate, Dana Marie Weaver, 16, July 12, 1949. Scott killed Weaver in a church parish house in Roanoke on May 8. With Scott are Al Knick, left, a guard, and J.P. Mullins, prison captain. (AP Photo/Richmond Times-Dispatch)

FIGURE 16. MUG SHOT of Lee Scott from Virginia State Penitentiary on his first arrival, July 12, 1949 (Library of Virginia)

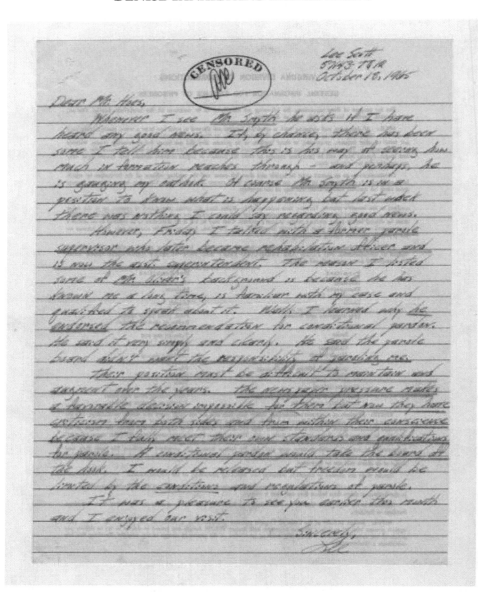

FIGURE 17. LETTER FROM Lee Scott written to Mr. Hoes from prison, dated October 18, 1965, as fully transcribed in Chapter 13 (Library of Virginia)

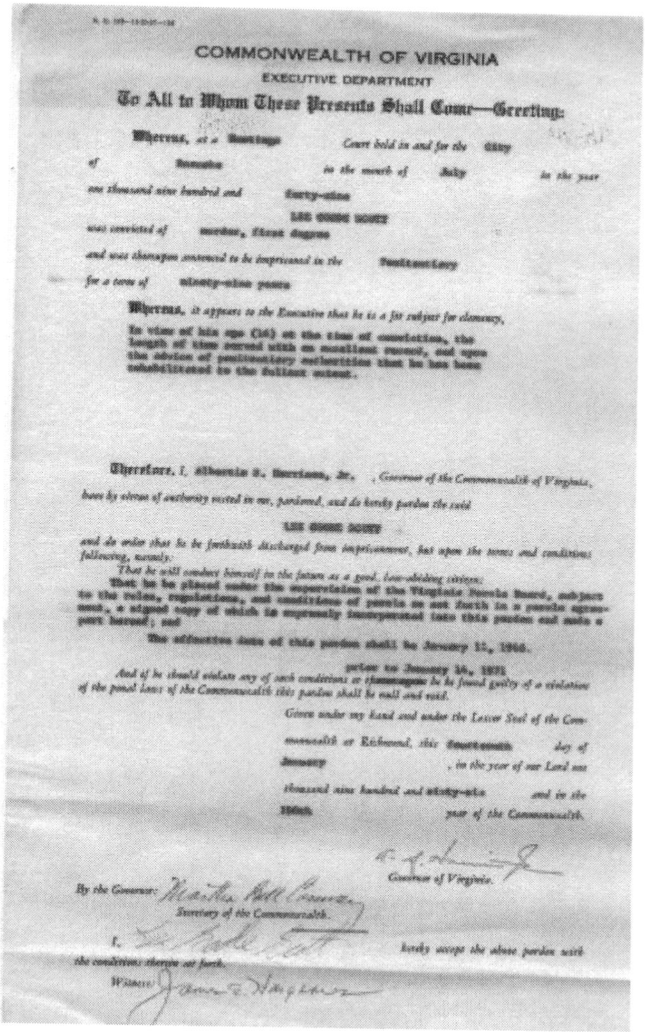

COMMONWEALTH OF VIRGINIA
EXECUTIVE DEPARTMENT
To All to Whom These Presents Shall Come—Greeting:

Whereas, at a Court held in and for the of in the month of in the year one thousand nine hundred and was convicted of and was thereupon sentenced to be imprisoned in the for a term of

Whereas, it appears to the Executive that he is a fit subject for clemency,

Therefore, I, , Governor of the Commonwealth of Virginia, have by virtue of authority vested in me, pardoned, and do hereby pardon the said and do order that he be forthwith discharged from imprisonment, but upon the terms and conditions following, namely:

That he will conduct himself in the future as a good, law-abiding citizen;

And if he should violate any of such conditions or he be found guilty of a violation of the penal laws of the Commonwealth this pardon shall be null and void.

Given under my hand and under the Lesser Seal of the Commonwealth at Richmond, this day of , in the year of our Lord one thousand nine hundred and and in the year of the Commonwealth.

Governor of Virginia.

By the Governor:
Secretary of the Commonwealth.

I, hereby accept the above pardon with the conditions therein set forth.

Witness:

FIGURE 18. LEE SCOTT'S pardon signed by Gov. Harrison (Library of Virginia)

FIGURE 19. THE LANDMARK Mill Mountain Star, photo by Russell Williams (City of Roanoke)

Selected Reference Sources

Books

Fields, Douglas (2015) Why We Snap: Understanding the Rage Circuit in Your Brain. New York: Dutton.

Harris, Nelson (2013) Hidden History of Roanoke: Star City Stories. The History Press.

Harris, Nelson (2021) The Roanoke Valley in the 1940s. The History Press.

Holmgren, Christer (2023) Cutting Point: Solving the Jack the Ripper and the Thames Torso Murders. Sweden: Timaios Press.

Lancer, Darlene. (2015) Codependency for Dummies, 2nd edition. Hoboken, New Jersey: John Wiley & Sons, Inc.

Macy, Beth (2016) Truevine: two brothers, a kidnapping, and a mother's quest: a true story of the Jim Crow South. New York: Little, Brown and Company.

van der Kolk, Bessel M.D. (2015) The Body Keeps the Score: Brain, Mind, and Body in the Healing of Trauma. Penguin Publishing Group.

Articles

Scism. M. R. "Children are Different: The Need for Reform of Virginia's Juvenile Transfer Laws," 22 Rich. Pub. Int. L. Rev. 445

Smith, Philip. "A Seemingly Endless Battle: Attorney Fights 25 Years, Without Pay, to Free Man," Washington Post, January 19, 1982

Steiner, Monica. "What is Parole? How Does Parole Work?" Nolo Press. https://www.nolo.com/legal-encyclopedia/how-does-parole-work.html

Special Collections

The Library of Virginia, Archives/Special Collections. "Secretary of the Commonwealth (RG13) Executive Papers, Accession 27212, Box 1518, Pardon records for Lee Goode Scott, 13 January 1966." BC 1172717; LOC: 04/E/009/008/07

The Library of Virginia. Archives/Special Collections. "Lee Goode Scott, Inmate #57143; State Penitentiary (RG 42), Accession 41558; Inmate Negatives, Box 277."

Roanoke Public Library, Virginia Room Digital Collection, The Acorn Jefferson High School Yearbook, 1949

Websites

- *Ancestry (online family tree, genealogy and public records research)* https://www.ancestry.com
- *Family Search (online family tree, genealogy and public records research)* https://www.familysearch.org
- *Library of Virginia (digitized historical newspapers)* https://virginiachronicle.com
- *U.S. Library of Congress (digitized historical newspapers)* https://chroniclingamerica.loc.gov
- *U.S. Library of Congress, Prints & Photographs Division, Online Catalog* http://www.loc.gov/pictures
- *Find A Grave (online collection of cemetery records and grave*

memorials) https://www.findagrave.com
- *State Archives at the Library of Virginia,* www.lva.virginia.gov
- *Historical Society of Western Virginia.* https://roanokehistory.org
- *Roanoke Public Library, Virginia Room, local historical archives and digital collections* http://www.virginiaroom.org/digital-collection/
- *The City of Roanoke, official civil government website, including tourism and visitor information* https://www.roanokeva.gov

Also by Denise Tanaka

Wish and A Star
Truth in Cinders
Lady in White
INTANGIBLE: Yasushi Tanaka and Louise G. Cann, A Marriage of Artist
and Author
Who Murdered Lizzie? My Family Story of the Brutal Crime of 1884 that
Shocked the City of Roanoke, Virginia
Flowers for Dana: the 1949 Murder of Dana Marie Weaver in the "Star City"
Roanoke, Virginia

Watch for more at sasorizabooks.com.

Also by Laurie Platt

Flowers for Dana: the 1949 Murder of Dana Marie Weaver in the "Star City"
Roanoke, Virginia

About the Author

Denise B. Tanaka has a lifelong passion for writing stories of magical beings and faraway worlds but is sometimes sidetracked by nonfiction projects. A graduate of Sonoma State University, she works as a senior paralegal in immigration law. She has dabbled in genealogy for more than 30 years and is very grateful for the internet.

Read more at sasorizabooks.com.